Advance Pr[...]
Bio-Tou[...]
Healing with the Powe[...]

"This is a wonderful personal narrative about the author's exploration into learning and practicing Bio-Touch, a hands-on energy healing modality. She gently weaves her personal story with the history and development of Bio-Touch. This is an interesting read for anyone drawn to explore an energy healing modality."

—**Dr. Ann Marie Chiasson**
Arizona Center for Integrative Medicine
Author of *Energy Healing: The Essentials of Self Care*

"Healing with touch is a tremendously powerful 'medicine.' Bio-Touch is a gentle, yet profound, approach that initiates deep healing in people. In this book, Debra Schildhouse masterfully introduces Bio-Touch to the world. Debra takes the reader on a journey of personal transformation, as she shares many fascinating stories of this simple, yet elegant, healing path."

—**Dr. BJ Adrezin**
Naturopathic Medical Doctor
Los Angeles, CA

"The story about Bio-Touch is one that needed to be told and Debra Schildhouse is the perfect storyteller to do that job. This simple, gentle, and loving technique has touched so many lives, and this book will touch so many more. Understanding Paul Bucky's journey will help you to understand why anyone walking into the Bio-Touch Center feels loved and everyone walking out feels better."

—**Dr. Bill Gallagher, DC**
DNFT® Chiropractor
Scottsdale, Arizona

"Bio-Touch has been an integral part of our healing retreats for families with children with special medical needs. It serves as a powerful tool for remembering that healing is in our own hands and that simple, loving touch can be transformative. Debra's heartfelt book is a reminder that we all can find the courage to pursue a healing journey, and that when we do, magic often happens."

—**Shay Beider**
Founder and Executive Director of Integrative Touch for Kids

BIO-TOUCH™

*Healing with the Power
in Our Fingertips*

Debra Schildhouse

Waterside Productions

IFBM
International Foundation of Bio-Magnetics
a nonprofit, tax exempt educational foundation
5634 East Pima Street
Tucson, Arizona 85712, USA
(800) 473-3812 • (520) 323-7951
International 001-520-323-7951

This edition published by Waterside Productions.

ISBN-13: 978-1-949003-62-8 print edition
ISBN-13: 978-1-949003-63-5 ebook edition

Book design by Janice Benight

Manufactured in the United States of America
10 9 8 7 6 5 4 3 2 1

This is a continuation of the copyright page.

The author will donate a percentage of the proceeds
from the sale of this book to the International Foundation of Bio-Magnetics
to support its mission of teaching Bio-Touch to everyone.

This book is dedicated to the memory of my father, Joseph J. NuDell, whose love still touches me every day, and to Lory, who taught me that compassion for others opens us to the many possibilities within ourselves.

Contents

Foreword

Gary E. Schwartz, PhD

Energy flows where the loving mind goes.

Is it possible that the simple practice of gently touching certain spots on the body can not only result in significant reductions in pain and suffering, but promote body–mind–spirit healing and health as well?

Moreover, is it possible that this simple fingertip touching procedure can be effortlessly practiced with minimal training, not only by undergraduate students, but yes, even young children as well?

Until I met Paul Bucky and learned about "Bio-Magnetic Touch Healing™," or "Bio-Touch™" for short, I would have said "of course not."

However, in the process of:

1. coming to know (and respect) him and his colleagues,

2. helping them conduct systematic survey research on Bio-Touch, and then

3. directly conducting research on Bio-Touch with students in my classes as well as in my laboratory (then called the Human Energy Systems Laboratory) I became convinced that Bio-Touch was all that they said it was, and more.

Then later, when Paul introduced me to Debra Schildhouse, the author of this beautifully written and deeply meaningful book about the history and promise of Bio-Touch for personal and global health, I was given the privilege of honoring her and Bio-Touch with this justly deserved introduction and commentary.

I should confess that I am a "biased" writer, not only because of witnessing the replicated evidence emerging from the research, but also from having spent many hours with Paul and his team "grilling them" on their history, motives, practices, and dreams. As you will see as you read this book, not only are Paul and Debra "unusual" people (to put it mildly), but the roots of the core Bio-Touch procedures are especially odd. Though I will not disclose any of these intriguing and challenging details here (you will have the fun of reading them in due course), I must acknowledge at the outset that the birthing and evolution of Bio-Touch is anything but conventional.

However, this unique history in no way alters the truth about the ease and effectiveness of the Bio-Touch procedures, nor does it alter the truth about the purity with which Paul, Debra, and certified Bio-Touch practitioners pursue this work. Their dedication is inspiring, and their combined efforts are humbling. And now, thanks to Debra's writing of this book, Bio-Touch has the potential to be appreciated and practiced worldwide.

I would like to take this opportunity to share two lessons I have learned from my involvement with Bio-Touch, especially as they relate to other healing practices that fall under the general rubric of energy healing. The first lesson is that it appears that there is no substitute for direct physical touch between the provider and the recipient. Though I have conducted research on the effectiveness of various non-contact healing practices including "distant intentionality" as reported in my book The Energy Healing Experiments, my research with Bio-Touch has clearly demonstrated that the strongest effects are consistently reported with direct skin to skin contact. This take home message is briefly discussed on the Bio-Touch website (http://www.justtouch.com/research-results-university-of-arizona-winter-2000-resurrecting-the-reputation-of-touch-a-presentation-by-paul-bucky-pres-ifbm-and-gary-schwartz-phd/) and a figure illustrating these results is redrawn below.

In brief, in this experiment a total of a 121 University of Arizona undergraduate students were recipients of three different "greeting" conditions (this condition is explained in Debra's book). One was "Skin-Contact"—direct physical contact between the provider's finger tips and the recipient's skin. Another was "Cloth-Contact" using the same finger

Ratings of Pain, Pre- and Post-Contact

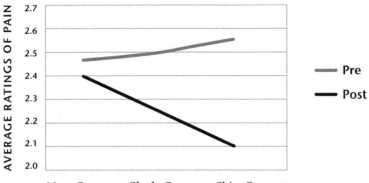

tips and body placements, but the provider's fingers only touched the recipient's clothing. Finally, the third was "Non-Contact" where the provider's fingers were a few inches away from the recipient's body.

The student recipients made ratings of pain using a 0–10 point scale both before (Pre – gray line) and after (Post – black line) each of the conditions. Each of the 121 students received all three conditions. Moreover, the "providers" were also university students who followed the simplest instructions about where to place their fingers. Since many of the students had minimal or no pain, it was not expected that large magnitude decreases in pain would be observed for the group as a whole.

Nonetheless, the data clearly showed that whereas "Non-Contact" had a minimal effect, and "Cloth-Contact" had a moderate effect, it was direct "Skin-Contact" that showed the greatest effect in terms of reducing reported pain following the procedure. These differences were highly statistically significant. In a word, direct physical touch mattered.

The question is, why?

Is the reason primarily physiological (for example, involving activation of the touch receptors via direct touch, including the warmth of the provider's fingers)?

Is the reason primarily psychological (for example, the positive feelings associated with gentle and safe touch)?

Or, is it possible that electromagnetic effects associated with direct physical contact are operating as well (for example, the actual sharing of electrons and current flow between the provider's heart / ECG and the recipient)? This possibility is illustrated in research reported in *The Energy Healing Experiments.*

My hypothesis is that all three mechanisms are probably involved in the process of Bio-Touch—physiological, psychological, and biophysical.

The second lesson is somewhat deeper and frankly more inspiring to me and maybe to you as well. The lesson relates to a theme expressed through Debra's book, the importance of love and the process of receiving and giving non-sexual loving touch.

The kind of love that Bio-Touch fosters is a high level of love, including empathy, compassion, caring, kindness, gentleness, protection, safety, warmth, gratitude, appreciation, and respect.

This is the kind of love that I emphasize in a workshop I regularly give at Canyon Ranch titled "Awakening the Power Within: Achieving Optimal Health through Energy Healing." I teach the guest the core principle, "Energy flows where the loving mind goes."

If you think loving thoughts about your hands—for example, you simply think "love heart" as you breathe in, and think "love hands" as you breath out—the temperature in your hands will typically and naturally increase. The reason is not because you are trying to "make" them warm, or are even that you are conscious that your hands are warming up. Your hands will warm up simply because (1) you are focusing your attention on them, and (2) you are doing so with loving intentions directed at them.

The "localization of mind focus loving energy" is implicitly involved in Bio-Touch, and it is explicitly nourished in Bio-Touch establishments. We might rephrase my statement slightly and say "Energy flows where the loving touch goes." The high level love that Bio-Touch fosters in its practitioners is palpable.

As you explore Debra's gracious and grateful book, my wish is that you become filled, as I did, with the wonder and promise that Bio-Touch offers all of us, our loved ones, the greater humanity, and nature as a whole.

GARY E. SCHWARTZ, PhD is Professor of Psychology, Medicine, Neurology, Psychiatry and Surgery, and is the Director of the Laboratory for Advances in Consciousness and Health at the University of Arizona. He is also Corporate Director of Development of Energy Healing at Canyon Ranch. His books include *The Living Energy Universe* and *The Energy Healing Experiments.*

Preface

I was skeptical when I heard what people said about Bio-Touch. It's a healing method that uses two fingers of each hand to touch specific points on the body, easing pain, relieving stress, and enhancing the body's natural healing ability. I had heard anyone could learn to do it. It wasn't even necessary to possess healing skills or talent. And apparently, everyone was effective on the very first attempt. That sounded too good to believe, and too simple to work. However, I was desperate to find a healing technique that I could depend on.

I had dabbled in a different kind of hands-on healing technique years before, helping a few of my "patients" feel better. It was thrilling to actually relieve someone's pain. But my method was unreliable, failing when I needed it the most—to ease my own daughter's misery. Jill contracted viral meningitis, and the intensity of her head and neck pain was too much for my limited healing abilities. Worse yet, her doctors' heavy narcotics were as powerless as my hands were.

After many hellish days, and two trips to the emergency room, Jill recovered. She was able to resume her busy life with no ill effects. But I felt raw and shell-shocked from the experience, never wanting to feel that helpless or hopeless again.

A year or so before Jill's illness, I had read an article about Bio-Touch. Its organization offered reasonably priced training classes at the Bio-Touch Center, which just happened to be located eight miles from my home in Tucson, Arizona. Though the healing method sounded intriguing at the time, I was busy volunteering elsewhere. So, I shelved the classes until sometime in the future when I would be less busy. Boy was that a lousy decision. Now I couldn't get to that center fast enough.

Unfortunately, on the first day of class I felt out of place among the other students, and even the instructors—all of whom I regarded as hippies and "tree huggers" of various ages. I could hear them talking about their dream journals, green diets, and spiritual studies. Heck, I didn't even meditate. What's more, I worried that the healing technique might turn out to be inappropriately weird. I had read that it was done by touching directly on the skin, so it was necessary for shirts to be removed before the healing session could begin. Being a modest woman, I was prepared to run out of that place the moment I felt naked in either the literal or the figurative sense.

But I relaxed when I heard the uplifting stories told by the three instructors. They explained how Bio-Touch, through its educational foundation, the International Foundation of Bio-Magnetics, had helped scores of people over the years by offering free healing sessions to anyone who walked through the center's door. They accepted donations only. Was I hearing things? Could such a place really exist?

When one of the instructors said students didn't need special knowledge, beliefs, or healing ability to use this technique effectively, I certainly felt qualified. And surprisingly, by the end of the first day of class, I was sure I was in the right place to learn the healing technique I was looking for.

All the practitioners who gave Bio-Touch sessions at their center were volunteers, and I now craved to join their ranks. So I completed the required classes, and an internship program, becoming a certified practitioner five months later. I was elated to be able to touch people, and ease their suffering every time I volunteered there.

But what I hadn't counted on was how much I learned about myself in the process. I was thrown into challenging situations that I wasn't prepared to handle. All I wanted to do at that point was run away from the center and never look back. Instead, with guidance from the Executive Director, Paul Bucky, and some soul-searching, I gritted my teeth and stayed, conquering my deepest aversions and fears in the process.

Years before I met him, Paul's severe backache had led him to seek relief from the local "healer" in a tiny town in Colorado. The man used Bio-Touch to relieve Paul's pain completely in two sessions. Paul recognized the untapped potential of Bio-Touch, devoting the rest of his life to volunteering as a practitioner and teaching it to others.

One day he mentioned to me how much he wished someone would write a book about Bio-Touch. He said people all over the world needed to read and learn about the healing technique that anyone could do, anywhere. He envisioned neighbors sharing Bio-Touch inside their homes in remote areas of China or Bangladesh, helping each other feel better.

His words sparked a sudden, overwhelming desire within me to be the author of that book. I didn't have professional writing experience; I wrote stories as a hobby. But that didn't seem to matter to the yearning that now burned in my soul. I was hungry to tell what I had seen and learned at the Bio-Touch Center.

I knew I needed to include background from Paul's life in my book. Besides having lived an extraordinary life, he had expanded Bio-Touch's reach well beyond the confines of Mancos, Colorado. He had created the foundation that offered classes to anyone who wanted to learn Bio-Touch, because it so perfectly embodied his lifelong creed to "love thy neighbor as thyself." And, he wouldn't rest until he shared it with many more people.

I spent hours interviewing him to uncover details about his unconventional life. He had been on a spiritual quest since his youth. In early adulthood, he invited friends to move into his house to embrace communal life. His home soon evolved into a self-sufficient community of residents seeking spiritual enlightenment as well as teaching it to others. Later, he lived in the mountains of Colorado in a one-hundred-year-old stone house without running water, gas, electricity, phone, or mail service. Eschewing modern civilization for four years, he and a select group of people lived as the pioneers had in order to fully concentrate on their spiritual studies.

I was touched, annoyed, amused, and sometimes grossed out by his depictions of past trials and triumphs. But the more I heard, the more I realized our lives had been on parallel trajectories for decades. Without living in close proximity, or even knowing each other, we had gone through the same experiences at the exact same point in time. It was something that neither of us could have imagined, considering our dissimilar backgrounds. Eventually, fate led each of us to the Bio-Touch Center in Tucson, Arizona, culminating in our ever-deepening friendship, as well as a shared vision for the future of the simple, yet powerful healing method called Bio-Touch.

CHAPTER ONE

My Wake-Up Call

One doctor makes work for another.

English Proverb

"Mom, my headache won't go away. I'm getting scared."

I gripped the phone as my daughter's voice sent waves of alarm through me. Jill's doctors had scratched their heads for three weeks trying to figure out what to do for her constant pain. It started as a low-level annoyance, but gradually increased in intensity. Now it was so bad, none of the prescribed medications could touch the throbbing. Even injections of heavy-duty painkillers were useless against her ongoing misery.

Jill was a healthy thirty-two year old woman who rarely got headaches. She'd never even experienced a migraine. But now, relentless pain encircled her eyes, creeping down the back of her neck. It was impossible for her to concentrate at work, enjoy social activities, or sleep through the night.

"Do you remember my friend Marc?" Jill's voice sounded thin and weak. "He's a neurologist. When I told him I had already seen two doctors for my headache, he came right over to do a quick evaluation on me. He said things seemed okay on the surface, but he wants me to go to the emergency room for in-depth testing."

"What kind of in-depth testing?" I asked, trying to keep the panic out of my voice.

"He said it was time for me to have a lumbar puncture," she answered. "Of course, I don't want to do that, but I told him if I'm not better by Saturday, I'll go for the test."

"A spinal tap?" I groaned. Visions of large needles protruding from my daughter's spine danced before my eyes.

"Yeah, Mom. He said it's the only way to see what's really going on with me."

"Well, I'm sure he knows what's best," I said, grateful that Jill couldn't see my look of horror. "Just concentrate on feeling better, okay sweetie?"

By Saturday Jill wasn't feeling better, so my husband, Howard, and I jumped in the car to drive one hundred miles from our home in Tucson, Arizona to Phoenix, where Jill lived. She was already at the emergency room. Our son, David, lived in Tucson, but happened to be in Phoenix that morning, so he drove Jill to the hospital.

Although Jill didn't think it was necessary for her dad and me to make the trip just for medical testing, we couldn't imagine being anywhere else. However, a half-hour outside of Tucson, the freeway traffic stood gridlocked due to an accident that occurred miles ahead of us. We endured forty-five minutes anxiously waiting in bumper-to-bumper traffic.

By the time we arrived at the hospital, the medical testing was over. David led us to a small room where Jill was tucked into a hospital bed. Her face and arms looked tiny, almost child-like, but her eyes were huge mirrors reflecting her distress. I gently took her hand in mine.

David explained that Jill had undergone an MRI, CT scan, and some blood tests. "Then they did the spinal tap," he continued, "but the doctor must have been new or something, because he kept inserting the needle in the wrong place."

"What?" I felt my stomach twist.

"Yeah, it took him three tries before he finally figured out the right spot," David answered. "It was pretty brutal. Now she's supposed to lie flat on her back for a while."

I broke out in a sweat, waves of nausea rolling through me. Howard inhaled sharply, his body tensing. I knew he felt like I did, wanting to find someone to demand answers of, but we kept quiet and calm so as not to upset our daughter. Somehow, we made light conversation until David left to drive back to Tucson. Howard and I walked David to the parking garage. When we returned to Jill's room, her emergency room doctor was standing next to her bed, chart in hand. He introduced himself, telling us that the results of the tests had come back.

"They were negative for everything that we tested her for," he said, removing his thick glasses to polish them with a dingy, frayed handkerchief.

"Well, that's good news, isn't it?" I asked.

"Oh, sure. Some nasty bacterial diseases have been ruled out," he conceded, "but we still don't have a definitive diagnosis at this point. And there's still one test we're waiting results on."

Howard looked wary. "What test is that, doctor?"

"The one for Bubonic Plague." His tone was as casual as if he'd said he just ordered a pizza.

"Wh . . . what? Didn't flea-bitten rats cause that in the Dark Ages? Where would Jill have picked that up?" I managed to ask.

The doctor cocked his head, as if stunned by my ignorance. "Haven't you read about it in the newspaper? We still have ten to twenty cases per year reported in this country—especially here in Arizona. But I wouldn't worry about it. I'm one-hundred percent sure she doesn't have Bubonic Plague."

"How can you be so sure?" Howard asked.

The man slid his glasses back onto his face, using a thick finger to push them up the bridge of his nose. His mouth spread into a dopey grin. "Because your daughter has had symptoms for weeks, right? If she had Bubonic Plague, she'd be dead by now."

A guttural sound escaped my lips. I opened and closed my fists a few times. The quick movements were solely to keep me from grabbing his stethoscope and twisting it around his throat until his eyes popped through his Coke-bottle lenses. Howard stood like a piece of granite, his reddening face an angry mask. The doctor cleared his throat, said he'd be back soon, and slunk away.

"What an ass," Jill whispered.

Hours later, now in her own bed, I watched her stare at the ceiling. I could see her profile clearly, illuminated by the soft glow of the wall lamp outside her bedroom door. When she blinked, her lashes fluttered like tiny fans.

"Mom? Do you see this forest growing all around me?"

"Huh? What forest?" I felt a flicker of alarm.

"Don't you see these trees sprouting up? Look. They've got mean faces, too." Her voice gurgled with wonder. "They're just like the ones who threw apples at Dorothy in *The Wizard of Oz*."

Though inwardly freaking out, I spoke in my calmest voice. "You're just having a dream, honey. You're sleepy from the medicine. I'll get a cool cloth for your head."

Over the years, no matter what was wrong with my kids, I always liked placing a damp cloth on their foreheads in addition to any other treatments they were receiving. I don't know if it helped them, but it always made me feel better. As I pawed through Jill's linen closet, I clucked my tongue with frustration. I couldn't believe she hadn't been given a diagnosis before being discharged from the emergency room. That jerk of a doctor had ruled out what she didn't have, but was clueless as to what she did have. So, he'd pumped her full of a variety of medications, while I was buried in sheets of paper scribbled with instructions regarding the correct dosages of the pills and liquids. Howard got the prescriptions filled at the pharmacy, picked up extra groceries, kissed us goodbye, and headed back to Tucson.

I had suggested that he go home, thinking I wouldn't need his assistance caring for Jill. I figured it would be no big deal to mother her back to health, alone. But I was dead wrong; I needed him. It was one-thirty in the morning, and Jill had been hallucinating for hours. She had also vomited twice. I assumed her system was ridding itself of that cocktail of prescription drugs, but who knew for sure?

When she threw up again, I called Jill's friend, Marc, the neurologist. I hated to wake him at that hour, but I was too concerned to wait until morning. As I dialed I was reminded of times gone by, when I called our pediatrician in the middle of the night for one child or the other.

Marc answered on the third ring. His voice sounded friendly and compassionate, containing just the slightest edge of sleepiness. He asked questions, then listened patiently to my detailed account of the past few hours. "After we hang up," he said, "get a flashlight, and shine it into Jill's eyes to check her pupils."

"Okay. But what should I be looking for?" I asked with dread.

"To see if her pupils are asymmetric. If one pupil is much larger than the other, or doesn't react to light, it would be considered an emergency. You would need to call an ambulance right away. But don't worry too much," he added, "I doubt that'll happen. And, please keep me informed of her condition."

I thanked him, hung up, and grabbed a flashlight. Jill flinched, trying to look away as I shone the light into her eyes. They looked normal. Then, not knowing what else to do, I crawled into bed with my daughter. It was the easiest way I could think of to keep up my vigil.

As I watched her, a bizarre pattern developed. She'd fall asleep for a few minutes, then awaken with a start, her eyelids popping open. When her eyes met mine, her face would register surprise. She'd smile, and ask why I was staring at her. Fresh pain would snake its way through her, she'd be sick in the wastebasket, and the cycle would repeat.

I prayed aloud for the strength and ability to cure my child. I closed my eyes, desperately trying to concentrate. Then I took some deep breaths, placing my hands on Jill's head. I visualized healing energy swirling around her, but after ten minutes, I was tired, and she was still hurting.

I'd been fascinated with the idea of hands-on healing ever since I saw a movie that Ellen Burstyn starred in back in 1980. Titled *Resurrection*, Burstyn played the role of a woman who had a near-death experience. She was injured in a horrific automobile accident. Her husband, the driver, was killed. While her body was clinically dead on the operating table, she floated into a vaporous tunnel that led to heaven. Deceased friends and family members pointed her toward a bright light. As she drew nearer to its brilliance, she felt great love within it. Then she was yanked back into her body.

She awoke in a hospital bed. The doctor explained that due to her injuries, she was now a paraplegic. She reeled from the trauma, grieving for her husband. Some months later, she sat in a wheelchair during a family picnic. Relatives panicked as blood gushed from a little girl's nose. The child was a hemophiliac. Her blood couldn't clot properly, so the nosebleed was life threatening. The woman insisted that the child sit on her lap. Without hesitating, she gently placed her hands on the little girl, stopping the flow of blood. The child was fine within minutes. The woman realized her hands were burning hot. That was the first hint that she now possessed the gift of healing.

Wondering if she might be able to help herself, the woman touched her paralyzed legs repeatedly, forcing herself to move with a focused determination. Soon she could walk again. As word spread about her gift, sick and injured people came to her for a chance to be healed. Many were. Sometimes she suffered physical agony as she transferred their pains and illnesses to herself. Burstyn's performance was breathtaking in its realism. According to newspaper accounts at that time, an authentic hands-on healer had been brought onto the movie set as an advisor.

As I stretched out on the bed next to Jill, I remembered how captivated I had been by the idea of "hands-on" healing after seeing that film. I'd found two books describing how to use my mind to direct healing energy into my hands; I practiced the required concentration exercises, hoping to feel the necessary heat entering my fingers, but that didn't happen very often. I loved it when it did, though.

I began to volunteer my newly acquired healing ability to any family members or friends who were bothered by the slightest headache or gas pain. First, I would inhale deeply a few times, trying to picture lights like laser beams shooting from my fingers. Then I would lay my hands on my "patient" wherever he or she hurt. Usually, nothing happened; neither of us felt a thing. I would silently scold my cold hands, chalking it up to my lack of mental focus. But when my hands did grow hot, I was often able to ease someone's pain. That made me feel terrific.

My most dramatic healing was the one I performed on my mother. Mom had a severe tooth infection caused by a failed root canal. She suffered with pain and swelling inside her mouth as well as on her face. Her left cheek and jaw were discolored and puffy. The inflammation caused her features to become so distorted that she was unrecognizable. Horrified, yet excited to try out my magic, I placed my hands on her face. In an instant, my fingers grew hot. I touched her for fifteen minutes, repeating the treatment several times that day. Before my eyes, her symptoms of swelling lessened, as did her pain. The tooth still needed to be extracted, but Mom was much more comfortable and looked normal by the time the oral surgeon saw her later that week.

Yes, that was a wonderful memory; I had felt like some kind of healing hero. But that was a long time ago. Unfortunately, I hadn't practiced that ability for years, and now my hands were cool and powerless to help Jill's headache. In fact, over the next few days Jill's pain grew even more intense. She could no longer leave her bed, except to crawl to the bathroom. When she tried to sit upright or stand, her head throbbed more fiercely than ever.

The emergency room doctor had explained that Jill needed to drink plenty of water after a spinal tap to avoid dehydration. But she refused most liquids offered to her because they made her nauseated. That was partly because of the medication and pain, but also because Jill's sense of smell had become acute. Normal odors from soaps and cleaning products, as well as cooking aromas from the kitchen, wafted through the house, turning her stomach. She ate very little.

Soon she couldn't bear to hear the slightest noise, either. Sound became amplified in her brain. Even when I turned a page in my magazine too crisply, it caused her pain. So I kept quiet, tiptoeing around the house like a mime. When I unloaded the dishwasher, I put away plates, glasses, and silverware in a slow-motion dance, trying to avoid the inevitable clinking, which is impossible to do, by the way.

From behind the closed office door across the hall from Jill's room, my delicate tapping on the computer keyboard created explosions in her ears. So there was no chance for my escape into email or Facebook. Listening to soft music or watching television was out of the question, too. Jill's sense of hearing had become superhuman.

As if things weren't bad enough, her eyes became overly sensitive. She couldn't tolerate the faintest sliver of light burning into her brain. All the blinds and shutters had to be pulled tight against the glaring Phoenix sunshine. After dusk I used as few lamps as possible, keeping the light bulbs clicked to their lowest settings.

We lived in a dark, quiet tomb cut off from the rest of the world. It was a maddening exercise in sensory deprivation. Yet, Jill wasn't improving. Her primary-care doctors and Marc wanted me to keep administering the pain medications while giving her body more time to heal. Well, how much time was it going to take? And what kind of alien creature was my daughter mutating into with her ultra senses of sight, smell, and hearing? I couldn't help comparing her to Jeff Goldblum in the movie *The Fly,* as he gradually morphed into the huge insect!

Countless times, I placed my hands on my daughter's head trying to force my mind to create healing energy. I couldn't do it; my stubborn fingers remained cold. But as frustrated as I was by my own failed attempts, the fact that Jill's prescribed pain pills weren't helping either made me want to scream.

Howard called several times a day. I'd carry my cell phone outside, or to the guest room, where I closed the door, huddled under the blankets, and whispered. Sometimes I just sobbed. I had never known such fear and dismay in my life. Many times my husband asked if I wanted him to come and help us. He was worried about our daughter, but didn't like how distressed I sounded, either. Lord knows how much I wanted him to come. But Jill was too sensitive to any stimuli. Howard was too energetic; not a tiptoeing kind of guy. It would have been hard on everyone, so I dissuaded him from coming.

I told him how much it helped just to talk to him, though. It also helped that Jill's friends and co-workers brought groceries, ran errands for us, and dropped cheery flowers, cards, and gifts at the front door. Jill permitted only one of her friends to come into her bedroom to see her. That friend had tears in her eyes when she left a few minutes later. She was shocked to see Jill in that condition, which made me feel even worse.

Each day I called Marc with updates on Jill's condition. He understood the difficulties, yet stressed the need for patience. But when I spoke with him on the seventh night of that longest week of my life, he told me we'd waited long enough for her to feel better.

"If Jill hasn't improved by morning, you'll need to drive her back to the emergency room for a procedure called a blood patch, which some patients require after a spinal tap," he explained. "It's obviously something her body needs; it's taking too long to heal on its own."

"Okay," I whispered, sickened by his words. Blood patch. How barbaric it sounded—as if they'd be using leeches or something. I tried to pay attention as he launched into an explanation, but I was preoccupied worrying how Jill would handle another painful procedure. Besides, I couldn't imagine getting her out of bed and dressed, let alone into the car. And how could she tolerate a bumpy ride in the brilliant light of day?

It was impossible to fall asleep that night with so much on my mind. I tossed and turned, praying that Jill would feel better in the morning. A flash of lightening startled me. Then the rumbling of thunder grew as the whoosh of rain hit the roof. I looked at the bedside clock. It was close to five in the morning on that fifth day of September—my late father's birthday.

Looking up toward the heavens, I whispered in the darkness, "Daddy, if you can hear me, I really need your help. Could you rally some angels up there? Jill is so sick. I'm terrified for her, and I'm feeling pretty sorry for myself, too."

Exhausted, I drifted off. Two hours later, I bolted upright in bed. It was still dark as night. Racing into Jill's room, I held my breath hoping to see a miracle. My heart sank. Her face was still pinched with pain.

I dragged myself back to the guestroom and looked out the window. Rain was falling in sheets; the sky wore a dark-gray cloak. I was surprised. A typical rainstorm in Phoenix came and went quickly, leaving little accumulation.

I dropped onto the bed like a ragdoll. Trying to psych myself up for what I had to do, I called Howard. In hushed tones I told him all the reasons it would be impossible to drag Jill to the hospital. He didn't accept my excuses. He insisted that I get her there, somehow, because the responsibility was mine to do so. I had to find the strength. In my sensitive state, I thought his words were harsh, but they were just the kick in the rear I needed.

I rushed through a shower before jumping into comfortable clothes. After choking down a few spoonfuls of instant oatmeal, I took a deep breath, and went to Jill's room. I whispered to her, saying that we had to go back to the emergency room. She protested for a second, but fell silent from weakness and pain. She managed to chew several bites of toast before I gently maneuvered her out of bed. Guiding her into clothes was easier than I expected, for some reason. We moved in a slow, but efficient dance, not wasting any of her precious energy.

Once we were outside, I was grateful for the heavy clouds shielding us from the sun's rays. That inky gloom became our protective blanket. After I eased Jill into the passenger seat of her car, I placed a small pillow under her neck, and sunglasses on her face, in case the sun suddenly broke through the downpour.

I started the engine, taking care as we rolled over the neighborhood speed bumps. The main roads were deserted. A few of the traffic lights were malfunctioning. Poncho-wearing police officers directed us through the puddled intersections, dotted with flares. Even though I drove thirty miles per hour to keep the ride as jostle-free as possible, we made it to the hospital in less than fifteen minutes.

When we arrived at the parking garage, I was surprised to see how few cars there were. I was able to pull into a space right by the entrance to the emergency room. We plodded to the door, Jill leaning against me.

It was quiet inside the waiting area. There were only a few people sitting on the benches. I knew that was unusual, especially for a weekend. And it was not just any weekend, but Labor Day weekend—a notoriously busy time for emergency rooms.

I guided Jill into a chair. Looking around for help, I recognized a nurse from the week before. His name was Michael, and he had cared for Jill with all the gentle compassion the doctor had lacked. When I called his name, he rushed over with a concerned look on his handsome face. I described what Jill had gone through all week, but broke down in tears before I could finish. Michael gave me a hug, assuring me he'd get Jill right into a bed. He sprinted away to grab a wheelchair.

After he'd whisked Jill to a room and helped her into bed, a doctor appeared. Thank goodness it wasn't the same one we'd dealt with last week. I was in no mood for him. This doctor's manner was warm, yet efficient. I felt myself begin to relax as he examined my daughter. He referred to her chart from the previous visit, then excused himself, and left the room. Michael hovered around Jill trying to make her more comfortable. Within moments, the doctor returned.

"Your daughter, unfortunately, is in the minority of people who need a blood patch following a spinal tap. She's continuing to leak cerebrospinal fluid from the holes that were punctured in her back during the spinal tap. The leak is causing her brain to literally sink down, pulling on the veins and causing her severe headache, nausea, and sensitivity to sound and stimuli. This will continue until the holes are plugged up, either by themselves or with a blood patch. It's taking too long for her body to plug the holes on its own. But once the holes are plugged, her body will make more spinal fluid and her brain will go right back to where it was.

"I called an anesthesiologist—a specialist—to do the procedure. He's one of our best, but he's booked solid with other patients. I'm afraid it'll be hours before he can take care of her," he explained. "I'm sorry. I know you've been through a lot, but that's the typical timeframe for a holiday weekend."

My eyes filled with tears again. "I understand. I'm just happy Jill will finally get some help," I sniffled.

The doctor placed his hand on my shoulder and handed me the tissue box. "I'll check back on both of you later. Everything's going to be fine."

After he left the room, I prepared myself for a long wait, settling into the chair next to Jill's bed. But, again, the doctor returned within moments.

"I've got great news," he beamed. "I just got a call from the anesthesiologist. He's had back-to-back cancellations, and is on his way right now to do the blood patch on Jill."

I felt like we'd won the lottery. While the doctor described how the blood patch would be performed, I forced my face to remain expressionless. After he left, Jill fretted about having to undergo the procedure. Who could blame her? Then she remembered that Rayna, a friend of hers, was an operating room nurse at that hospital. She asked Michael if he could find out if Rayna was on duty that morning. He left the room to page her.

When he returned a few minutes later, Rayna was behind him, dressed in scrubs. She rushed to Jill's bedside and held her hand. She said she was sorry to hear how much pain Jill had endured all week, and assured her that the blood patch would help.

When the specialist arrived, I was asked to wait outside the room. I knew Jill was in good hands with Michael, Rayna, and the doctors, so I didn't fall apart while walking the halls. I called Howard.

"It's so different than when we were here last week, honey," I marveled. "Everyone is treating us so well. We seem to be in a state of grace today. They're doing the blood patch procedure now."

"So she really needs to have it, huh?" His voice was thick with worry. "How is it done?"

"Yes, it's necessary. After she had the spinal tap last week, too much of Jill's spinal fluid leaked out, causing all her odd symptoms," I explained, pausing to take a breath. "They're taking a small amount of blood from her arm, and injecting it into the spinal tap site on her back. That blood will form a patch to cover the holes that the other doctor made in the outer membrane of her spinal cord. It'll restore her pressure to normal. She should have immediate relief."

"Is the procedure done often? It sounds awful. But if it works . . ." Howard's voice trailed off.

"The doctor said that up to fifty percent of patients experience that kind of headache after a spinal tap, but most of those folks are helped by pain medications. Jill was unlucky enough to be in the minority needing a blood patch."

Just then, Michael appeared in front of me, smiling. He said that it was all over, Jill did well, and I could come back in. As I ran down to her room, I told Howard I would call him back.

"Your daughter should start feeling better very soon, now," the anesthesiologist announced as I burst in.

I watched in amazement. A smile slowly spread across Jill's tired, but beautiful, face. What a glorious moment! I closed my eyes, giving a silent prayer of thanks. Rayna and Michael hugged me as tears dripped down my cheeks.

The anesthesiologist immediately raised the head of Jill's bed, and started a mild pain medication, intravenously, to keep her relaxed. She was thrilled to be able to sit upright without pain. I grinned at her, trying to forget that the damned spinal tap had caused her so much misery in the first place. I just focused on the fact that she was pain-free now, and everything had gone our way since we left the house that morning.

Two hours later, Jill was discharged from the hospital. I walked next to Michael as he pushed Jill's wheelchair down the hall. The waiting room was now teeming with people. Every seat was taken. The rain had stopped, the sun had emerged, and life had reverted to normal, once again.

Michael helped Jill into the car. We each hugged him goodbye. And as we drove into the glorious sunshine, it was a thrill to look at my daughter and see her face relaxed instead of twisted in agony. My heart was bursting with gratitude for the unusual rainstorm, the empathy shown by Michael, Rayna, and the doctor, and for the skill of the anesthesiologist. I also felt a deep appreciation for Marc's knowledge and support. When he called later that day, Jill was happy to tell him she'd been pain-free since leaving the hospital hours earlier.

The next morning, I awoke from a great night's sleep. Dashing into Jill's room, I prayed she'd still be comfortable. She was sitting up in bed, stretching.

"I'm starving!" she announced. "Let's go out for breakfast."

We threw on clothes, excited as children. Jill drove us to her favorite waffle house. When we walked through the front door, the aromas of sizzling meat and brewing coffee enveloped us. Instead of being sickened by it, Jill inhaled it, deeply.

We devoured crispy bacon, velvety scrambled eggs, and gooey waffles. It was wonderful to sit there like normal people, eating, laughing, and enjoying those simple pleasures. We were a bit sensitive to the noise and high energy of the restaurant after living in virtual isolation for a week. But no one could tell that by looking at our smiling faces; no one could have guessed the kind of nightmare we'd just lived through.

Jill never received an official diagnosis. Marc believed, though, that she had viral meningitis, because bacterial meningitis would have made her a lot sicker than she was. Marc expected that the spinal tap would show a high white blood cell count and lots of lymphocytes which fight viruses. But the extracted fluid was clear, which sometimes happens because not everything shows up perfectly in spinal fluid. Because there was neither bacterial nor viral meningitis visible, the results were inconclusive. Jill's illness had run its course over a few weeks. When she finally recovered, and her headache—a symptom of viral meningitis—ceased, we couldn't tell because that's when she began to suffer from side effects of the spinal tap, that caused headache pain and her other severe symptoms.

Thank heavens Jill was able to go right back to work, moving on with her busy life as if nothing had happened. But my life had forever changed after that gut-wrenching fear had crushed me for seven interminable days and nights. I had glimpsed the place in hell that parents visit when they don't know if their child will recover. So, I made a solemn vow: I would find a way to insure I'd never feel that helpless or hopeless, again.

CHAPTER TWO

A Whole New Experience

Nothing in life is to be feared. It is only to be understood.

Marie Curie

Quotation widely attributed to Marie Curie

I could almost hear my nerve-endings crackling in my ears as I drove. I was headed to my first class to learn the healing technique called Bio-Touch. Upon returning to Tucson after Jill's recovery, I immediately called the Bio-Touch Center and signed up for one of their upcoming courses. I'd read about Bio-Touch a year before, and though the idea of taking classes fascinated me, I shelved the idea, figuring I could do it sometime in the future. Well, the future came a lot quicker than I bargained for.

What a lousy decision it had been to postpone exploring the touch-healing technique I had read about a year ago!

As I waited at a red light, I drummed my fingers on the steering wheel. Something I read on the class instruction sheet, mailed to me the week before, had me anxious. In fact, I felt so jittery, I toyed with the idea of turning the car around, and forgetting the whole thing.

When the Bio-Touch envelope had arrived I tore it open, excited to read whatever crucial information was inside. After clearing my throat, I stood in front of my husband—a born skeptic—and read parts of the letter aloud.

"It says here that the two-day, basic practitioner training class is only forty-eight dollars. Wow, that's pretty reasonable, huh?"

Howard nodded with a grunt.

I continued reading. "Students will learn how to find specific healing points on the body, and touch those points using the first two fingers of each hand. Bio-Touch is practiced by touching directly on the skin so participants will remove their . . . um . . . their . . . shirts." I hurried on, bracing myself for his reaction. "Women are encouraged to wear a two-piece bathing suit top or a brassiere for the practice sessions."

Howard had been sitting at the kitchen table eating lunch and reading the paper on that peaceful Saturday. But as my words sunk into his brain, his head jerked up, swiveling on his neck like a ruffled owl. "What? Are you kidding me? You have to take your clothes off for this class?" He swallowed hard, placing the sandwich he'd been munching back on his plate. "You aren't going to remove your shirt in front of some weirdoes in this class, are you?" His eyebrows bristled, angry little bushes above his glasses.

Before I could answer, he took a deep breath to calm himself. "Look, I understand how much you want to take this course. But what kind of healing technique requires you to remove your clothes? That doesn't sound legitimate, does it?"

I crossed my arms, remaining stiffly silent.

"All right," he conceded, noting the look of resolve on my face, "just promise me that you will never take your shirt off in front of any male students or healers, ever, okay?"

"Of course I promise, honey." I smiled at his predictability, hugging him as he sagged with relief. "You know I'm modest. I don't relish the thought of parading around in my bra in front of people . . . let alone strange men."

"Yeah, well, I'm still not feeling good about this whole thing. It sounds shady," he warned, shaking his head.

I would have been surprised if he hadn't protested at the thought of random men seeing me in my bra. Throughout our marriage, Howard had felt compelled to protect my modesty—adamant that any state of my undress was for his eyes only—unless I needed a medical doctor. He had always drawn the drapes or pulled down the shades when I got in or out of clothes, even if I stood far from the windows. One time, in a high-rise hotel room in Waikiki, he caught sight of me wriggling into my bathing suit in preparation for the beach. Without missing a beat, he dashed to the large picture window, yanking the curtains closed as he stumbled over his own feet.

"For heaven's sake, Howard. We're on the sixteenth floor! Who in the world can see me?" I shook my head at his silliness.

Shrugging his shoulders, he mumbled something about window washers. I was never quite sure if I should be flattered or insulted by his compulsion to shield my body from sight, but it always made me laugh.

I wasn't laughing, though, as I drove to the Bio-Touch Center that beautiful autumn day. Howard's warning echoed in my ears. What if he was right and the healing technique was bogus? What if I really was about to spend the day with a group of half-naked kooks?

I found the address I was looking for, and as I pulled into the parking lot, I was relieved to see several empty spots close to the front door—in case I needed to jump back into my car for a quick getaway. The building, a single story structure, was painted soft coral with blue accents. A purple Bio-Touch sign beckoned from above the windows.

Glancing at my watch, I saw that I was fifteen minutes early. I debated whether to stay in the car, but I took a deep breath, and made my way to the front door. As I opened it, I heard the soft tinkling of chimes. Stepping inside, I inhaled a spicy scent coming from a pot of brewing tea. The pleasant fragrance mingled with the doughy aromas of cakes and cookies that sat on a platter near the teapot.

I was alone, so I tiptoed around the room, taking everything in. Hawaiian-sounding music played softly from the speakers of a stereo system. A large, wooden bookcase held a variety of health and wellness books. On the other side of the room, there were additional wooden shelves that displayed vitamin supplements, teas, and soaps for sale. The concrete floor was beautifully etched in a tiled design, and the walls were painted in bold colors of purple, turquoise, red, and mustard. There were two comfy-looking couches as well as a dozen or so chairs that had been arranged in a large circle. A bald-headed female mannequin—the kind you'd see in any department store—stood at the front of the room draped in a colorful wrap. I did a double take, wondering what she would be used for, when a smiling woman suddenly appeared from a back room.

"Hello. I'm sorry I didn't hear you come in. Welcome to the Bio-Touch Center. I'm Sandy."

"Hi. I'm Debra."

She penciled something on a clipboard, and offered me some refreshments. Just as I reached for the bright green grapes, the front door opened. Several women breezed in chattering to each other. Sandy greeted them by name, joining their conversation. Feeling like the outsider I was, I made my way to one of the couches. It felt cushiony enough, but I sat as rigid as a flagpole, holding my body as close to the over-stuffed arm as possible. I placed my purse next to me so no one could sit too close.

More students arrived. Soon the room vibrated with the chatter of three men and nine women, ranging in age from twentysomething to eighty. From my perch, I could see how they were all "new age," earthy, tree-hugger types. They were dressed for comfort in over-sized tee shirts, and baggy, relaxed shorts. Their flip-flops slapped against their heels as they walked. I was clad in a crisp, raspberry-colored blouse, pressed slacks, and high-heeled sandals. The women wore little, if any, jewelry, nail polish, or make-up. Adorned with all of the above, I stuck out like a pink-iced donut among bagels.

I overheard snippets of conversation, including the use of kale in smoothies for vegan diets, the best time to meditate, and the importance of wisdom journeys, whatever those were. Boy, was I in the wrong place. I was still digesting my bacon omelet breakfast, I didn't meditate, and I didn't know a wisdom journey from a wisdom tooth.

A woman appeared before me. She smiled and nodded, making herself comfortable on the couch next to my purse. I flashed a tentative grin, and then looked away; I didn't feel like engaging in conversation with anyone yet. It felt safer to surround myself with a protective wall. I tried to relax, but my leg muscles felt tight, ready to spring into action if I needed to bolt. My right heel bounced with nervous energy.

While the other students laughed and chatted with each other, I sat wondering how soon we'd have to take our shirts off. And as my jumpy foot kept its vigil on the floor, I pictured myself shirtless, running to the car, peeling out of the parking lot, and speeding home. Howard would be waiting at the door for me, wearing a look of justified righteousness.

Sandy walked to the front of the room, joined by another woman and a man. The trio introduced themselves as Sandy, Chardonai, and Tod, our instructors. With a smile, Tod informed us that he spelled his name with only one 'd.' Then he asked us to introduce ourselves, and say a few words about why we were there. I focused my attention on the teachers, carefully listening to every word they said. My senses were heightened, alert for continued signs of "normalcy." At that point, I had psyched myself up enough to dash out the door if anything freaky started happening.

Each student, in turn, announced their name, then explained what they were hoping to get out of the class. Several of them mentioned that they had benefitted from having Bio-Touch sessions in the past, and wanted to learn how to share the technique with others. When it was my turn to speak, my face grew warm as all eyes rested on me.

"I'm Debra, and I'm here to learn a reliable healing technique, because my old one didn't work when my daughter was sick a few weeks ago."

Chardonai nodded and thanked each of us for sharing. "We're going to be together for six hours today and six more tomorrow, so we'll be getting to know each other pretty well," she said with a playful smile on her lips.

Little bursts of laughter broke out around the room. My heart skipped a beat. I worried just how we were going to be getting to know each other so well. As I looked around at the others, I envied how relaxed they looked, their faces full of anticipation.

After giving us a basic explanation of the purpose of Bio-Touch, and a brief history of its origins, the teachers shared their personal experiences as certified practitioners. Each of them described how they had literally and figuratively touched the lives of people who were sick or in pain. They spoke of their gratitude at being in the position to help others. They each choked up as they relayed how they benefitted as much, themselves, as the people they touched. Their stories seemed heartfelt, and their tears genuine, so I let myself relax a bit. Still, I couldn't help wondering when we'd all start singing *Kumbaya*.

"Unlike other touch-healing methods, with Bio-Touch you don't have to have any special knowledge, state of mind, or spiritual or religious beliefs," Chardonai stated. "There are no levels of ability to master, and no hierarchy within the organization. Everyone is effective the very first time they touch."

Was she really saying people were effective the very first time they touched using this method? So, we could touch someone today and help heal that person? If that were true, it would be incredible, but I wasn't convinced. Still, it was nice to know they weren't going to insist that we believe in meditation or veganism.

"The center is run by volunteers, as it's always been," Tod explained, "and many of those volunteers have been with us for years. We never charge for Bio-Touch sessions; we've always given them on a donations-only basis."

What? Free healing sessions? That sounded even more unbelievable to me. How could they keep such a nice facility without charging for their services?

"By the way," Chardonai interjected, "nurses taking this class will receive twelve continuing education units of credit. This class has been approved by the California Board of Registered Nursing and by the Arizona Nurses Association."

Well, that sounded legitimate. My muscles relaxed even further.

"Bio-Touch often reverses years of pain and inflammation due to chronic diseases," Tod added. "I like to compare it to the peeling of an onion. After a session, the body begins to shed what it doesn't need, becoming healthier and healthier. You've all heard the warnings about the latest flu bug expected this winter? Well, it doesn't scare me." He held up his arms extending the first two fingers of each hand into the air. "I say, bring it on. These fingers are all we'll need!" His face looked triumphant.

For the first time that day, I felt a flicker of hope run through me. Bio-Touch sounded like it worked. But I still had no idea how the technique was actually done. For all I knew, it was like those shows I had seen on TV where the evangelist smacks the ill person on the forehead, yelling, "You are healed!"

"Does anyone have a question at this time?" Tod asked, his eyes scanning the room.

My heart pounded as I raised my hand. "Yes. How, exactly, is this technique done?"

Everyone turned to look at me. "You've never had a Bio-Touch session?" one of the students asked, a stunned look on her face.

I shook my head, feeling like the only woman in the room wearing white after Labor Day. And that's when I got to hear how every other student had experienced Bio-Touch at least once. Most of them enjoyed sessions on a regular basis. As they took turns speaking, some revealed that they were licensed practitioners of healing techniques such as massage therapy, acupuncture, reflexology, kinesiology, and others I had never heard of. They were taking the class so they could add Bio-Touch to whatever healing methods they were already offering their clients.

"Bio-Touch is unique . . . I can't think of any healing technique that feels more relaxing and loving, and my clients sure need that," said a student in a dreamy voice.

"I feel the same way," said another. "During a session, I start feeling like life's okay and I'm okay. It's just touching with two fingers from each hand; yet it's a wonderful expression of acceptance and love."

As I looked around, I saw that everyone was smiling and nodding their heads in agreement. I forced myself not to roll my eyes as it occurred to me they sounded as programmed as the robots from the movie *The Stepford Wives*. How could they feel loved and accepted just by being touched with a few fingers? What was the big deal? It's not like we were discussing a nice, brisk rubdown or even a satisfying back scratch—something that I could get excited about. And what did love and acceptance have to do with healing, anyway?

Chardonai and Tod began handing out copies of the Bio-Touch manual, the training book describing the philosophy and technique. It was paperback, simply bound, and slightly larger than the size of notebook paper. We were told that the accompanying DVD would show actual practitioners touching recipients using the correct sets of points for specific conditions. I opened the book, noticing the mission and vision statements at the bottom of the first page:

> *Our mission is to teach Bio-Touch, an application of the*
> *universal principle 'Love thy Neighbor,' as a means to alle-*
> *viate pain and stress, and support good health through all*
> *stages of life.*

Our vision is to encourage all people to take responsibil-
ity for their own health care, empower them to assist oth-
ers, and create a community of people worldwide dedicated
to service, self-awareness, and recognizing the equality of
all humanity—thus forming a chain which shall go on
indefinitely.

That sounded impressive, though I didn't really understand what the term "self-awareness" meant. Wasn't everybody already aware of themselves? And there was that word "love" again, too. Wasn't healing more about physiology than emotion?

As I thumbed through more pages I saw the location of touch points were shown on easy-to-understand, black and white drawings. There were also photographs of actual recipients being touched. The instructions used crystal-clear phrases like "located at the big bone at the base of the neck" instead of medical terminology.

Further into the book was a page of terms, along with their explanations. The person who performed Bio-Touch was referred to as the practitioner or associate. The person who received the session was called the recipient.

There was also a section called Suggestions for Addressing Specific Conditions. It listed over fifty medical issues that a practitioner might encounter, and the minimum areas of the body to work on. Many of the conditions were serious medical problems, but the manual implied that Bio-Touch could help them. Oh, how I wanted to believe that was true.

Tod walked over to the mannequin and ripped off her wrap. She was naked underneath. Her plastic skin was chipped here and there, and a few of her fingers had broken off. I took a deep breath, hoping things weren't about to get very strange.

Tod said, "The Bio-Touch technique consists of seventeen sets of points that address specific diseases or symptoms. For example, there are six points on the neck that are touched when someone is suffering from a tension headache, neck pain, or soreness of the upper back." He demonstrated how to find the precise points for several medical conditions, using the mannequin as his recipient. As he touched the dummy, I could see the necessity of her naked state, as it gave him unrestricted access. For each medical condition, Tod touched different areas with his fingertips; he made it look simple.

When he finished, we had a fifteen-minute recess to stretch our legs and enjoy the array of refreshments. I watched my couch neighbor serve herself, then sit back down to eat. On a whim, I babbled to her about having worked up an appetite. I glanced at her nametag as Robie Jean smiled and recommended the lemon squares.

"I hope you all enjoyed your snacks, but now it's time to divide the class into groups of four students each, so please listen for your names," Tod announced. "Each group will proceed into one of our three session rooms. One instructor will be joining each group, and we'll begin practicing the touch points on each other. So, bring your manuals with you."

My heart pumped faster as names were called and groups were formed. My name was included in a group with two women and a man. My eyes darted from face to face searching for negative reactions from the other women. But no one else seemed bothered, in the least, about having a man in their group. How was that possible? Was I the only modest person there? Howard's solemn face popped into my mind. I could hear him asking me to keep my promise.

"Excuse me," I called out, "I need to be in an all-female group." Apparently, that was an unusual request. Heads whipped around, amused eyes zeroing in on me. "My husband would be more comfortable," I explained, "and so would I."

"That's not a problem at all," Chardonai said in a reassuring tone. "The comfort of each individual is of the utmost importance here at the center."

I breathed a sigh of relief as my group was reassembled into an all-female one, which included Robie Jean. Sandy, our assigned teacher, reminded us to use the sinks to wash our hands before working on each other. It was an essential first step of the healing technique.

With clean hands, we entered one of the session rooms. Sandy joined us, sliding the door shut behind her. I liked the cozy space with its soft lighting and teal color on the walls. In the middle of the room a massage table stood, covered with a spotless sheet.

Sandy asked for a volunteer to be the first recipient. "As you all know by now, Bio-Touch works through skin-to-skin contact only," she pointed out. "That's why recipients remove their shirts . . . to make it easier for practitioners to reach their mid-sections and backs. Bras can be left on."

My eyes widened. Did that mean some women removed their bras for a session? I couldn't imagine being so uninhibited.

Robie Jean removed her shirt and slipped it over a clothes hanger on the wall. I was relieved that she chose to leave her bra on. I only hoped that everyone would; I wasn't ready to touch topless women. Robie Jean hopped on the massage table, sitting up straight so we could take turns "greeting" our first official recipient. That meant that we each, in turn, extended the index and middle fingers of our dominant hands and touched her on a specific point, called the "greeting point," in the fleshy area just beneath her breastbone.

"This solar plexus area is the power point of the body," Sandy explained as she pointed to its picture in the manual. "It's always the first way a practitioner connects with the recipient. Hold that touch for six to eight seconds—very lightly—as if a butterfly landed there. Then, take your dominant hand again, and touch this point at the back of her neck holding it lightly for six to eight seconds as well. The two points that make up the 'greeting' set of points will then be completed."

That sounded simple enough, and it was easy for the other students in the room. They were a bit clumsy with their greetings, but their enthusiasm made up for it. However, when it was my turn to greet the recipient, my heart raced. I could feel my breathing becoming quick and shallow. A wave of nausea washed over me as I broke out in a sweat—my usual reaction to serious stress. How was I going to touch this person on the skin of her mid-section?

I never had a reason before this to touch someone I didn't know in such an intimate way. Granted, I struck up conversations with strangers in stores or at the post office. I even touched them on the arm while sharing a joke or story. And I had always been "touchy-feely" with my husband and children. I delighted in hugging and kissing them, and having them respond in kind. But the thought of touching someone I just met on their bare breastbone area was too weird for me.

Forcing myself to stay calm, I remembered how much I wanted to learn this technique. So I gritted my teeth, willing my trembling hand to move toward the woman. She was brave enough to smile. But as my frosty fingers connected with her warm skin, she flinched. I jabbered an apology.

After managing to touch all the points correctly, it was time for me to remove my shirt and take a turn as the recipient. I unbuttoned my blouse with trembling fingers. This had to be the strangest thing I had ever done in my life. I made sure my bra was firmly in place before climbing onto the table. I closed my eyes, dreading the fingers that would soon touch my vulnerable middle.

Although Robie Jean's hands were warm, I shuddered as she touched me. She seemed at ease as she found the two greeting points, then moved to the back of my neck. I began to relax in spite of myself. As her fingers landed on areas beneath my skull, and along my shoulders, I was amazed at how good it felt. So good, in fact, that I began to like her and everyone else in the room. I chuckled to myself. Maybe I was feeling that love and acceptance the other students referred to earlier.

By the time the training course ended the next afternoon, I was surprised at how close I felt toward several of the students in the class— especially Robie Jean. I didn't think it was possible to bond with strangers in only one weekend. But my protective wall crumbled into a million pieces as we learned Bio-Touch together, ate our lunches on the back patio, and shared stories about our lives and families.

As we hugged goodbye, Robie Jean said, "I really enjoyed watching your transformation this weekend, Debra."

"Oh?" I answered, pretending not to know what she meant.

"Well, yesterday you were sitting at the far end of the couch with your arms crossed tightly in front of you. It was a clear message for everyone to leave you alone," she recounted, her blue eyes twinkling. "It was fun to see you gradually warm up to Bio-Touch . . . and to us."

I smiled, but felt ridiculous realizing how obvious my fears and defensiveness had been to everybody. Worried that things might deteriorate into the "too-bizarre-for-me" category, I was ready to run away. Instead, I gained life-changing knowledge while meeting interesting people I would never have met, otherwise. Those other students and I differed in many ways, but the only thing that mattered at the Bio-Touch Center was our similarities.

I was proud of the certificate of completion that I, along with the others, received that day. We were now practitioners of Bio-Touch. The certificate stated that it was awarded by the International Foundation of Bio-Magnetics (IFBM), the organization that teaches and shares information about the methods of Bio-Touch. My name was printed in the center, stating that I had successfully completed the Bio-Touch practitioner training and demonstrated a sincere desire to help relieve the suffering of humankind.

Now I knew the basics of Bio-Touch, and along with the manual as a guide, I could help people feel better. But I wanted to learn so much more, so I signed up to take the four day advanced training course to become what is called "a graduate practitioner." Those classes, starting in a couple of weeks, would take place over two consecutive weekends.

Singing with the radio on the drive home, I felt at peace knowing I had found the perfect healing method. It was exactly what I was looking for, and I couldn't wait to delve even deeper into its mysteries. But I knew I should curb my enthusiasm, a little, before walking into our house. Although I described to Howard how well the class went the day before—and he was relieved to hear it—I didn't want him to suspect that I was somehow brainwashed by "those weirdoes" at the Bio-Touch Center!

CHAPTER THREE

Acknowledging My Past

Everyone grieves in different ways.
For some, it could take longer or shorter.
I do know it never disappears.
An ember still smolders inside me.
Most days, I don't notice it,
but, out of the blue, it'll flare to life.

—Maria V. Snyder
Storm Class

This time as I drove to the Bio-Touch Center for a training class, I felt like I belonged there. I was dressed in a plain white tee shirt and black velour tracksuit. My feet were happy inside comfy sneakers. The only jewelry I wore was my wedding ring and some tiny pearl earrings. However, I still sported my makeup and perfume. My beloved cosmetics were a part of me . . . something I wasn't willing to give up, even to fit in at the Bio-Touch Center.

After parking my car in the back lot, I strode toward the patio. A slightly built man of average height was standing by the door. His thinning grayish hair matched his well-trimmed beard. When he saw me, he smiled, flashing vibrant blue eyes. I returned his smile, wondering if he was Paul Bucky. I heard about him at my first training class.

"Hello. You must be Debra," he said.

"I am. And are you Paul?"

"Yep, that's me. Nice to meet you."

"You too, but how did you know who I was?" I asked.

His smile turned devilish. "Oh, I heard all about you."

"Uh oh. I can only imagine. But did you hear what I looked like, too?"

"Oh, just something about big blonde hair and lipstick," he said. "Welcome back. Come on inside." As he gestured for me to enter the back door, I got a feeling of déjà vu. Had I met him before?

As I stepped inside, I heard ukuleles twanging from the stereo speakers, despite the chatter of gathering students. The aroma of baked goods made my stomach growl. I was happy to see Robie Jean and another student I knew from the previous class. Choosing my usual roost next to the arm of the couch, I let my body relax as my hands cupped a mug of hot tea and a chocolate chip cookie. On the floor next to my feet sat my purse, politely making room for Robie Jean to sit next to me.

Tod and Chardonai, our instructors from last class, seated themselves in the chairs at the front of the room. Paul soon joined them, making himself comfortable in the middle chair. Immediately he addressed the class, introducing himself as the Bio-Touch co-founder and Executive Director. It took a few seconds for the room to grow quiet as every head turned in his direction. Tod and Chardonai followed his lead, introducing themselves, then asking the students, one at a time, to do the same.

With the introductions complete, Paul regaled us with stories from his past. In the 1980s, severe back pain forced him to seek relief from a man named Norman, a hands-on healer in their small town of Mancos, Colorado. Norman actually devised the Bio-Touch technique. He used it for years to help suffering people, welcoming them into his home for sessions.

"And that's my story . . . if you choose to believe it," Paul said, a teasing smile on his face.

"What do you mean?" one of the students wanted to know.

"Well, some people don't believe Norman ever existed." Paul's eyes danced. "They think I made him up—that I'm the one who really came up with the technique."

"Well, did you?" a student piped up.

"Maybe," Paul shrugged, "maybe not. Our certified practitioner in Cairo, named Shahrzad, believes that Bio-Touch was actually practiced seven thousand years ago in Egypt. She's seen hieroglyphics and other ancient artifacts in a Cairo museum showing people using the same two fingers of each hand that we use. They were touching others at the same greeting points that we do. So, the mystery continues but the most important thing is the technique itself—not its origin."

Maybe it was the tone of Paul's voice, or how his expression suggested there was so much more beneath his unassuming exterior, but I was curious about him. The few snippets he'd shared about his unconventional life fascinated me; I wanted to hear more.

He stopped talking long enough to sip water from a green plastic bottle. "And of course," he continued, "the concept of self-awareness is a very important aspect of Bio-Touch. It is the awareness of oneself in relation to one's surroundings. The first step to becoming self-aware is to quietly observe your own reactions to different circumstances. Then it just grows from there. Any questions?"

I wanted to ask him why becoming aware of my body's reactions to things was so important, but I chickened out. I had the feeling that everyone else in the room already understood that concept, and I didn't want to be the dunce of the class.

"Why do you think this healing method works? Isn't it too simple to really be effective?" a student asked, leaning forward in his chair. "Could it just be the placebo effect?"

"I don't know why it works," Paul answered, his eyebrows rising comically. "Nobody really knows why this method works. We just know that it does, from our own experiences as well as through the results of various research studies. Yes, it is simple. Its beauty is in its simplicity. And if it is the placebo effect, that's great, too. The placebo effect is real, acknowledged by even mainstream medicine."

"Does Bio-Touch ever heal someone right away? Like, immediately during or after a session?" another student wanted to know.

"Yes, I've seen many instances of that over the years. But normally, it'll take regular sessions, given over a couple or several months, to slowly make a difference. Certainly, on some level it does help every recipient immediately, because, as research has shown, it reduces their stress level and increases their feelings of well being."

Students blurted out questions, pushing for further explanation. From the look on Paul's face, it was obvious he was pleased with what was being asked. His ease at answering hinted at how often he'd addressed those same questions over the years.

"The basic purpose of Bio-Touch is to persuade the body to bring itself back into harmony, by utilizing its own natural, inherent healing abilities," he explained. "These classes are designed to teach you how to assist that natural healing process. But as certified practitioners of Bio-Touch, you will never diagnose conditions or make medical recommendations. Also, you'll never ask recipients about their belief systems or challenge their current health care programs. Bio-Touch works so well in conjunction with standard medical protocols, all you'll need to do is . . . just touch."

Looking at the wall clock, Tod got to his feet to announce that it was time for a brief recess. I was glad, because my stomach was growling. I joined the students who were congregating around the refreshments. As I devoured a slice of poppy-seed cake, I could sense a buzzing excitement in the room. It felt pleasant—as though waves of energy were undulating from person to person as we chatted.

Soon Paul was telling us to grab our training manuals. We were headed into the session rooms to practice a few sets of points on each other. Apparently, another thing he'd heard about me was my need to train with women only, because when he called names to form groups, my name was included in an all-female one. And Chardonai was our instructor. What a relief! The promise I made to Howard about not letting any male students or instructors see me shirtless, wouldn't have to be re-announced.

As we practiced on each other, I willed my memory to sharpen up. I wanted to absorb which of the points were effective for what medical conditions, and how to pinpoint each one. I knew it would take time to learn them all, but I was frustrated with myself whenever my mind came up blank.

I enjoyed learning how to do the sweeping-like movements used for extra enhancements around the regular points. I just let my fingers glide any way that felt right to me. It was fun until I jabbed one of my student recipients with my fingernail. It only caused a light scratch, and she laughed off my apology, but I was embarrassed that I couldn't control my fingertips. I made a mental note to fish out the emery board from my makeup bag so I could file my nails down to stubs.

When we finished practicing, we rejoined the other students in the main room. At that point, the instructors raised questions that led to discussions on various aspects of spirituality. Death and dying, and the possibility of life after death, were some topics explored. We were all invited to share our feelings, as well as any personal stories relevant to the discussions.

Some people recounted humorous tales of deceased relatives, and I laughed along with the other students. But some shared painful experiences, moving many of us to tears. One woman told of her young daughter's illness and death some twenty years earlier. In many ways she was still trying to accept it and find inner peace.

Another woman's adult daughter ran away from home years before. It was impossible for the woman to put that nightmare behind her, because she never found out what happened to her daughter—whether she was alive or dead.

I was stunned by the depths of anguish those people lived through, and in awe of the courage it took them to share their stories with a roomful of new acquaintances. As they were speaking from their hearts, I found myself thinking about my own painful story. I, too, had lost loved ones many years before, suffering trauma that shattered my life. But since I rarely spoke of it to anyone—let alone people I hardly knew—there was no way I was ready to share it with the class. I remained silent.

The following Saturday was the third day of the four-day course. I was sitting at a round, white table on the patio behind the Bio-Touch Center, chatting with Robie Jean and two other students. It was a cool, yet sunny day, perfect for eating our lunches outside.

"Would anyone at this table like to share what triggered their interest in healing others?" Robie Jean asked our group, between forkfuls of her salad.

The woman sitting to my right spoke up. She described her childhood pain and fear while living with an abusive father and an ill mother who was too weak to protect her children from their father's torments.

"Even as a kid of eight or nine, I knew both my parents were sick. I wished so hard that I could heal them," she said, shaking her head.

"That must have been so challenging," I said, unable to fathom that kind of misery.

"Yeah, it was a tough way to grow up. But that's where my desire to heal others came from," she said biting into her sandwich.

The woman across from me began to speak, then. Her story involved an angry, alcoholic husband who enjoyed beating on her for a decade. She finally got the nerve to leave him, and after years of therapy and healing, wanted to help others who were in pain.

Robie Jean looked at me. I averted my gaze, chewing on a carrot stick. She smiled, and began telling us about her difficult childhood, painful divorce, and consequent strained relationship with her adult children.

As I looked at the faces of the women around that table I realized how much I trusted and respected them. They'd dragged through the trenches of life, pulling themselves up to be of service to others. I knew I was safe sharing my story with them.

I was nervous as I heard the first words trickle from my lips. Then pent-up pain spewed like a burst dam over their lunches. They sat motionless as I shared my story. I told them that when I was young I had a boyfriend named Loryn, whom everyone fondly called Lory. I deeply loved him for the two years we'd gone steady. One Friday evening in October of 1972, he went for a drive around town in his new car. His best friend, Henry, accompanied him. I wasn't with them because I was attending a sorority get-together.

Sometime after midnight, as they traveled on I-75 in our hometown of Cincinnati, Ohio, Lory must have dozed off. Apparently, Henry was also asleep for a while, having adjusted the back of his seat to the reclining position.

The car suddenly slammed into a sign pole at the side of the road. Because Henry was not wearing a seatbelt, he was ejected from the car and instantly killed. Lory, wearing his seatbelt, was still alive in the mangled car. An ambulance brought him to the hospital where he was rushed into surgery. But the doctors weren't able to save him. Because of severe internal injuries from the impact of the steering wheel, he passed away before the sun came up.

Lory and Henry were just eighteen years old. I was nineteen, and up until then, my world was a warm and wonderful place. But suddenly I was trapped in a stone-cold, surreal nightmare as I stared into the open casket of the beautiful, young man that I loved. He looked like he was asleep—peaceful and perfect—showing no visible signs of the trauma he'd gone through. There wasn't a scratch on him that I could see, which made it all the more impossible to accept. He didn't even look hurt. How could he be dead?

One of Lory's close friends, Larry, saw my fingers reaching toward the casket. I was scared to touch Lory, but I felt compelled to. Larry took my hand and gently placed it on Lory's chest, telling me that it was okay . . . I didn't need to be afraid. But my fingers recoiled when I felt how unnatural and hard his body was. My mind screamed that this couldn't be happening, but I knew then, that Lory—the amazing spark that was Lory—was no longer in that body. And I shuddered as the planet turned icy without his light to keep it warm.

Larry led me away from the casket. I stared at the way people's lips moved beneath their red-rimmed eyes, as they tried to find something comforting to say. But there were no words to soothe the sharp edges of my grief.

The funeral home was so crowded with the bereaved that it was standing-room only. That was because Lory touched many people in his short life. He was a kind young man who went out of his way to make people feel special. Sometimes, though, I found that trait annoying. Even when we were in a terrible rush to get someplace on time, if he noticed someone he knew—whether they were young or old, a good friend or just an acquaintance—he'd stop to chat with them. It was important for him to take a minute to ask how they were doing. I would sigh and cluck impatiently to myself, but in my heart, I knew I was witnessing a depth of compassion unusual in someone so young.

One chilly, rainy Saturday night, Lory drove us downtown after a date. We cruised around for a while, but by eleven o'clock the wet streets were deserted, and it was time for him to drive me home. That's when he caught sight of a man staggering on the sidewalk, soaked to the bone.

"I'll be right back," he said, as he pulled the car to the curb. He hopped out his door.

As I watched my boyfriend sprint over to the man, I couldn't imagine what he was doing. The next thing I knew, he opened the back door, and helped the guy into the car. When Lory saw the look of shock and disgust on my face, he took my hand. Smiling in the way that always melted my heart, he said, "It'll be okay. I promise."

He drove slowly, calling out street names to help the old fellow remember his address. I sat in horror, covering my nose as the car's interior began to reek of booze and filth. We finally pulled up to the right place. Lory got out, helped the man go through his pockets to locate his keys, led him up the steps of an apartment building, and made sure he got safely inside his door.

Jumping back into the car, Lory leaned over to give me a big hug. His hair dripped rainwater down my neck. "That poor old guy might have died out in this weather," he said, as we pulled away from the curb. I didn't answer, though. I was too busy opening the windows, inhaling the fresh, clean breeze.

Not only did I adore Lory, but I also came to love his family. I spent a lot of time hanging out at his house. Lory and I watched television, snacking and laughing with his mom, dad, and three sisters. Their home vibrated with the energy of all those personalities. We'd visit his grandparents often, too. They all went out of their way to make me feel like I was part of their family—something I had hoped to be someday. But now I could only stand beside them in mourning, sharing the depth of their pain.

My mother was the one who had broken the news to me about the accident after hearing it on the local news. Knowing that it would be the hardest thing she had ever done, she drove to my sorority house early that morning, sat me down, and looked at me as she gathered her strength. I knew whatever she was about to say would be bad. But it was so much worse; it was inconceivable. The next thing I knew, mom was driving me to Lory's house. I looked out the car window observing the passing scenery and wondering why things still looked normal.

People were going on about their lives as if nothing had happened. Didn't they realize the world had changed forever? Couldn't they sense the encroaching darkness? When Lory's mother, Roz, opened the front door, she immediately pulled me into her arms for a hug.

"Thank God you weren't in the car with them," she said, her voice thick with grief.

Even though I was young, I was able to appreciate how difficult that must have been for her to say. My mother, now in her mid-nineties, still refers to those words as the most admirable and loving ones she ever heard in her life.

After the funeral service, the hearse and several black limousines led the long caravan of cars to the cemetery. It took time for all the mourners to walk through the sprawling grounds to Lory's gravesite. My parents walked next to me, each holding on to one of my arms. I kept my eyes down, watching the brittle, fallen leaves swirl in the wind.

As we began to climb the cement steps that jutted from the hillside, my father stopped to catch his breath. His face turned ashen as beads of sweat formed on his forehead. Dad had been in fragile health for several years after suffering two minor heart attacks. He struggled with angina pain, especially during stress or physical exertion.

Worry clouded my mother's face as she asked my father if he was all right. She touched Dad's arm, peering into his eyes. That's when I noticed how frail he looked and how much he'd aged. I could feel the fear blossom along the length of my gut.

"Don't you die on me too, Daddy. I couldn't take it!"

His blue eyes flickered with pain. It was angina pain, but I'm sure my words hurt him, too. Somehow, though, he found the strength to reassure me.

"Don't worry about me. I'm fine." His voice sounded hoarse. After placing a nitroglycerin pill under his tongue, something I'd seen him do many times, we resumed climbing the steps. Slowly we trudged on toward Lory's gravesite.

I tried to convince myself that Daddy would be okay; he was just taking Lory's death hard, that's all. He was a strong man—surely he had strength enough to overcome his health issues. After all, dad was a paratrooper with the 101st Airborne Division, the Screaming Eagles, in World War II. Jumping out of planes and gliders, he had dodged his share of deadly shrapnel. He was a medic, too. While tending to injured soldiers during the invasion of Normandy, a bomb exploded near him, embedding fragments of metal above his right eye. But his sight was spared, and only a faint scar remained. He was awarded the Purple Heart.

He then survived being captured by German troops at the Battle of the Bulge in Bastogne, Belgium. Along with many other American soldiers, he was forced to march for three hundred twenty five miles—in deep snow and record-breaking cold—to a prisoner of war camp in Germany. During the march, hundreds of men died from illness, exhaustion, and hypothermia. Prisoners were beaten with rifle butts, slashed with bayonets, or even shot if they marched too slowly or stopped to rest.

When Dad arrived at the camp, his feet were frozen. But somehow he was able to withstand the rigors of that hellhole for four and a half months. Although thirty pounds lighter, he was able to make it home in one piece, bringing one of the bayonets that a prison guard used on him, as a souvenir.

He lived by the words of his favorite saying, "Winners never quit and quitters never win." So I prayed that he would continue holding tight to that motto, and would keep fighting his illness. I absolutely adored my father; I had always been a daddy's girl. And with Lory gone, I needed his love and strength even more. He just had to be all right.

But Dad wasn't all right. Six months later he, too, was dead. He suffered a fatal heart attack on April 29, 1973. He was only fifty-six years old. Weeks later, somehow functioning through my agonizing grief, I paged through his old war scrapbook. I gasped at the irony as I read one of the yellowed newspaper articles that had been written about him. April 29th was also the date, back in 1945, that Russian soldiers liberated Dad from the prisoner of war camp.

I took a deep breath as I finished speaking. Then I shrugged, trying to smile as I looked at the faces of my new friends. Their lunches sat untouched as they wiped away tears.

"I can't believe you lost two such important people in your life within six months of each other," Robie Jean said, "and you were just a teenager. Obviously that's what triggered your desire to help people heal." She drew me into her warm arms for a nice, long hug.

The next day, I proudly received my second certificate of completion. By having the two weekends of further training classes, I had now advanced to what is called a "graduate practitioner" of Bio-Touch. But there was still more I wanted to learn, and one more certificate that I was determined to receive—that of a certified practitioner. As a certified practitioner, I would be able to volunteer at the center after my sixty-hour internship was complete.

Thirty years earlier, when I watched that hands-on healing movie, *Resurrection*, I was haunted by questions—questions that still burned within me. What if I had known how to perform a healing method like Bio-Touch when I was nineteen? Could I have reversed the damage to Lory's internal organs or at least lessened his pain before or after surgery? Would I have been able to improve the condition of Dad's hardened cardiac arteries? And the most tormenting question of all . . . could I have helped prolong their lives?

Of course, I would never know the answers to those questions. I didn't know about Bio-Touch then. But I knew about it now, and I knew how to use it to ease people's suffering, even if their lives couldn't be extended. Never again would I have to pace around someone in misery, feeling helpless and hopeless like I did during Jill's illness. Instead, I could give Bio-Touch sessions, helping my recipient, as well as myself.

CHAPTER FOUR

Seeing It Firsthand

It is only through touching one another (not just physically)
and observing what we reflect for each other
that we are able to know ourselves. We remind
each other of who we are. This is our purpose.

Jacquelyn Small

Becoming Naturally Therapeutic

On a sunny morning two weeks later, I jumped out of bed excited to be starting my internship toward becoming a certified Bio-Touch practitioner. After showering, I gave myself a manicure, filing my fingernails down so short, they hurt. Then I applied glossy white polish. Even though I would be observing rather than touching anyone that first day, I figured my nails should look clean and harmless.

I slipped into the fresh clothes I had chosen the night before, like a kid on the first day of school. Checking myself in the mirror, I hoped my pants, shirt, socks and sneakers—all pure white—looked appropriate. I had no idea why I wanted to wear the color of a doctor or a virgin, but somehow it felt right.

Breathless with anticipation, I arrived at the Bio-Touch Center almost twenty minutes early. I burst through the front door hoping to show everyone my enthusiasm, but there was no one in the main room. I could hear muffled voices coming from the session rooms, though, so I busied myself around the reception desk. I opened a drawer. Recipients' charts, filed alphabetically inside of manila folders, flopped forward in front of my eyes. I picked through a few of the charts, trying to make sense of them. Then, worried that someone might think I was snooping, I shoved them back into the folders, and shut the drawer.

Looking around, my eyes rested on the wipe-off board on the wall that showed the names of all the interns. Next to each name, a number was written indicating the hours they had volunteered toward that sixty-hour target of becoming certified. Some of the names had the numbers thirty, forty, and even fifty written next to them. Meanwhile, my name sported the lowly number one beside it. And that hour had been given to everyone who had attended a pre-training class. I longed for the day I could grab the green marker attached to that board, and change my number to the magic number of sixty.

Finishing the internship is not a race, I reminded myself. Everyone volunteered according to his or her own schedule and comfort level. Still, I was nosy enough to follow other interns' logged hours, and I was sure they'd be watching mine as well. Maybe it wasn't a race, but I sensed a hint of competition, anyway.

I looked at the shelves where nutritional supplements, teas, soaps, books, and other products were offered for sale. A sign posted above explained that those items were specially priced for members of the non-profit Bio-Touch organization, the International Foundation of Bio-Magnetics. The yearly membership fee was only eighteen dollars. I could see that by collecting money for membership dues and class tuition, Bio-Touch was able to sustain itself without charging for sessions—something I had wondered about.

The front door chimed open a few times as recipients began arriving for their appointments. I felt jittery as I greeted each of them. I sat on the swivel chair behind the desk, hoping the phone wouldn't ring. I didn't know the official way to answer it, yet. Trying to look busy, I read over some printed material that was pinned to the wall. Out of the corner of my eye I watched recipients browse through the books on the library shelves. Others helped themselves to hot tea, sipping as they relaxed on the couches.

Then in quick succession, two of the practitioners emerged from the session rooms. After welcoming me, they turned to give goodbye hugs to the people they had just worked on. I could see how relaxed the departing recipients looked; their bodies had a loose fluidity to them. They smiled as they sailed out the front door.

Minutes later, Paul came through the back door. He strode over to the desk, stopping in front of me. "Good afternoon, Debra," he said in a spirited tone. "Are you ready to get started?"

"I sure am." I answered with more confidence than I felt.

"Great. Wash your hands and you can join me."

As I lathered up, I wondered why I was doing so. I was sure the teachers said we would only observe our first day. My heart thudded at the prospect of touching a recipient so soon.

Paul and I walked into the session room together, but I remained glued to a spot next to the closed door. Paul smiled and chatted with the recipient, touching the silver-haired man at the greeting points. When he'd finished, he beckoned me forward. With a sinking feeling, I realized he had no intention of letting me merely watch that day.

"Debra, come and meet Al," Paul said in a cheery voice. "He gave his permission to have you practice on him. We always ask for our recipients' okay before having an intern work on them," he explained.

"Oh, good," I lied, filled with dread. "It's nice to meet you." I tried to smile and figure out where the exact greeting spots were on Al's body at the same time. Paul gently corrected my poor attempts.

"Al comes in for maintenance sessions on a regular basis. He doesn't have medical issues or much pain, and he wants to keep it that way."

"Yeah," Al bantered, "for someone my age, that's important. Sorry I don't have more wrong with me for you to practice on, Debra. As it is, Paul must be bored working on me every week."

"Actually, in over twenty years, I've never been bored while giving a session. Not once. But if it ever does get boring," Paul added with a shrug, "I'll just go do something else."

Not knowing if he was joking or not, I watched in amazement as he touched Al. With his fluid sweeping movements, precise touch points, and relaxed confidence, I couldn't imagine him going off to do anything else. After working each set of points, he encouraged me to follow suit. I tried to touch the right spots, but my clumsy efforts needed to be adjusted every time. At one point, I was horrified to see white pressure marks appear briefly on Al's skin from my heavy-handedness. He didn't seem to notice, but Paul did.

"Don't worry," he consoled. "The ability to touch lightly will come with practice."

Al slumped forward, sighing with relief as the back of his neck and shoulders were worked on. And when he stretched out on the table so his back could be touched, he relaxed into a mound of pliable putty.

"Thank you, Al," Paul said when the session was over, demonstrating a pleasant and respectful way to finish. I parroted Paul's words.

As we walked out the door, I glanced back at Al. He looked like a melted candle on that massage table. A few minutes later when he emerged from the session room, Al appeared refreshed and ready to head back out into the real world.

Paul updated Al's chart, checking off which sets of points had been touched during that session. Then he showed me the correct way to answer the phone, make appointments in the book, and prepare the session room for the next recipient. Dirty linens in hand, I followed him out the back door to the area on the patio where the washer and dryer stood. After tossing the sheets into the clothes hamper, I helped Paul fold a load of laundry that was still warm from the dryer.

Soon we were washing our hands again to prepare for the next recipient. As before, Paul had gotten the recipient's permission to have an intern present. As we entered the session room, he smiled at Barbara, chatting with her as he touched her greeting points. He signaled for me to come closer.

As I fumbled about trying to find the right greeting areas, I realized why it was so tricky to do so. The differences in size and shape between people's bodies created the need to adjust where those points were found on each person. And those points had to be touched precisely and lightly—two things that were way beyond my ability at that time.

Barbara was a fit, forty-ish looking woman who enjoyed hiking. But pain and weakness in her knees prevented her from enjoying her hobby. Paul showed me how to touch and sweep my fingers all around her knees. As I copied his motions, I found myself appreciating the amazing marvels-of-engineering that knees really are. In fact, that was the day those over-burdened body parts became my favorite areas to work on.

The afternoon passed in a pleasant blur. Then, while Paul and I worked on his next recipient, my fingers grew toasty warm as I applied the sweeping motions. That hadn't happened with the previous two recipients, but now the warmth seemed to rise up in waves around me. Even though it was uncomfortable to be that hot, I was happy for such an obvious sign that my fingers were finally generating heat—something they weren't able to do for my daughter when she was so sick. And the best part was that I didn't have to focus my mind to force energy into my hands. It was just happening on its own.

Soon though, I felt drained, and my back was stiff. Paul must have noticed my wincing face as I tried to stretch my spine.

"You need to position yourself closer to the massage table as you work," he advised. "Look where you're standing."

I glanced down, surprised to see how far my body was from the table. I must have been straining all day, extending my arms to reach the recipients from that distance. To my own detriment, I had attempted to respect personal boundaries—theirs as well as mine.

Paul smiled as I inched nearer. "You'll get used to being so close to the table and to the recipients."

What a relief it was, at the end of the day, to write on the intern chart that I had volunteered for four hours. As I drew the number, my head spun with all I learned, and all I was required to remember. But as I drove home, I basked in the pleasure of knowing I helped people feel better that day.

For the next few months, studying the training manual and trying to memorize the correct locations of all the touch points became my nightly routine. I also watched the accompanying DVD, which helped cement those points in my mind. I knew surprise quizzes would be sprung on me at the center, and I wanted to be ready for them.

During my internship, I was reminded to never give medical advice or try to diagnose a recipient's condition. Many recipients had already been given a diagnosis from their medical doctor. We were there to listen to them and to 'just touch.'

I was taught that pain was not the only thing that brought recipients to the Bio-Touch Center, although it was the number one complaint. Unrecognized stress was the biggest hidden problem for many people.

They didn't realize how stressed out they were, or how that stress was overwhelming their immune systems and causing them pain and illness.

By touching specific spots, we were able to help relieve headaches, neck and back aches, tooth and gum pain, ear aches, shoulder aches, arthritis pain, and a variety of conditions of the legs, knees, ankles, feet, and toes. We also helped alleviate chest congestion, digestive issues, skin conditions, and sinus miseries.

We soothed the pain from old injuries, new injuries, sports injuries, muscle strains, migraine headaches, and pinched nerves. Even various discomforts associated with autoimmune diseases such as lupus and fibromyalgia were eased.

Paul taught me how to look for curvatures of spines, skin discolorations, bruising, and other issues. But this was done strictly for us to know where to apply additional touching, not for any diagnostic purpose. He also explained that places where people felt pain in their bodies wasn't necessarily where that pain originated. For instance, if someone had pain in their wrist or hand, the source of that pain could well be in their neck. So, we would address the neck area, as well.

I learned that for the average recipient relief lasted from a few hours to a few days following the first Bio-Touch session. With subsequent sessions, the relief lasted longer and longer. Often, regular weekly sessions seemed to address the root cause of people's pain and other symptoms. Though some recipients continued to have residual pain or discomfort after their sessions, most didn't need to take as much medication as they did before.

Although I enjoyed learning from Paul the most, I also gained valuable insight and confidence when I worked with other certified practitioners. Each of them had their own unique styles. They all were precise when touching the points on the body, of course, but they had adopted their own ways of using sweeping-like movements and other enhancements. Because they had their own distinct personalities, they all related to their recipients in different ways. Some were more energetic and talkative, while others were calm and quiet, letting the recipient determine the level of conversation. I paid attention. It was important to learn how to decipher a recipient's clues as to whether they wanted to chat or preferred to enjoy their session in a state of relaxed silence.

But I wondered why neither Paul nor the other practitioners ever mentioned growing too warm while working on a recipient. In fact, they all seemed cool and collected, while I was a hot mess. One day, while fanning my face with my hand, I asked Paul what my problem was.

"Everyone's different when it comes to sharing Bio-Touch," he explained. "It's a very individual thing. In your case, you get overheated. That's how it affects you. Realizing that is just another way you're growing in your own self-awareness."

There was that self-awareness concept again. Why was it so important to be aware of how sweaty I was? Then it dawned on me that if I was that toasty while we were in the midst of winter's chill, how miserable would I be giving sessions in the summer? Tucson temperatures reached into the triple digits many days from June until October. I could only hope that the air conditioning system at the center was in better shape than I was.

I was anxious to use my new skills on anyone who needed them, so I gave some sessions to friends and family members at home. Tara had recently undergone an emergency appendectomy. She had recovered, but was left with several small abdominal scars from the laparoscopic surgery. I invited her over for a session, telling her that Bio-Touch could reduce the appearance of scars, whether they were recent ones or not.

As I was touching her, my hands grew even hotter than normal. In fact, the heat traveled up my arms and spread into my chest, throat, and face. I felt like I was on fire. Interrupting the session, I swept my hair up into a clip, trying to cool my sweaty neck.

"Wow. Your fingers are so hot, they're burning me," Tara said, as I resumed working.

Concerned, I yanked my hands away from her body. "Burning you?" I asked, concerned. "I'm sorry. For some reason, I'm like a radiator today. Do you want me to stop?"

"No, it's okay. Keep going. It just felt weird . . . almost like you touched me with a hot match."

The next day when I got to the Bio-Touch Center, I told Paul what had happened, and asked him if it were possible to burn someone during a session.

"There's no possibility of inflicting a real burn, but it's not unusual for fresh scars like hers to be ultra-sensitive, especially if you're giving off that much heat," he answered.

A few days later Tara called me, her voice filled with excitement. "I just got back from my post surgery check-up with the doctor. She couldn't believe the advanced state of healing my scars were in, already. And do you remember that little ball of scar tissue that you could feel under one of my scars? Well, that's completely gone! I'm impressed. Thank you."

I was elated because Tara was a registered nurse, so her amazement with Bio-Touch was all the more gratifying.

One afternoon Howard came home early from work, complaining of severe pain in his neck. He didn't know what was causing it, but the pain was so intense he couldn't sit in front of his computer a minute longer.

"I'll give you a session and ease it," I offered. But he balked at the thought of having the painful area touched. I don't think he was convinced yet that Bio-Touch was worth his time. "Come on. Sit here on the couch. I'll turn the TV on so you won't notice what I'm doing," I insisted.

I sat next to him, working on his neck as he flipped channels. He found a ballgame to capture his attention for fifteen minutes or so, before becoming restless. He thanked me for my effort, but I could tell he wasn't expecting much benefit from it. A few hours later, though, he admitted that the pain had lessened. It was easier for him to move his head from side to side.

"Okay, I'm a believer," Howard conceded the next morning. "I slept great and the pain's gone."

"Well, I'm glad to hear that," I said, chuckling at his mystified expression.

Our son, David, injured his shoulder at work, after lifting something heavy. The doctor prescribed pain and anti-inflammatory pills with an order for physical therapy to follow. I told David to come over to the house and I would give him a session.

"Hey," he complained when I had finished, "why is the pain more intense than it was before?" He grimaced as he adjusted his shoulder. "Did you do something wrong?"

"No. That happens sometimes. I'm sorry, honey. It won't last long." I knew that after a session, an injury could feel worse, temporarily, as the healing process sped up.

David was leery about Bio-Touch after that first session. But after a few physical therapy visits, and a few more sessions with me, he acknowledged that his shoulder was as good as new.

As the months flew by, and my volunteer hours added up on the intern chart, I realized that I was no longer tired at the end of each four-hour shift. If anything, I felt invigorated. I wasn't sure if Bio-Touch was energizing me as I worked on recipients, or if I had just gotten used to my new routine.

Finally, on March 5, 2010, which just happened to be my mother's ninetieth birthday, I reached my goal. I accepted my newest certificate with its shiny gold seal, authorizing me as a certified practitioner of Bio-Touch. Filled with excitement, I seized the green marker, writing that magic number of hours on the chart as big as the space would allow.

I couldn't stop staring at my official name tag after Paul placed it in my hand. As he wrote my name in the scheduling book, I peeked over his shoulder, dancing a little jig. Now, recipients could make appointments with me, and I could work on them by myself. I could use my knowledge and fingers to make people feel better on a regular basis!

However, there was one particular set of touch points—out of the seventeen sets that make up the Bio-Touch method—that Howard had asked me to never perform. On men, that is. It was the lower abdominal set, used to address conditions such as colitis, constipation, hernias, infertility, and bladder issues. That set was performed using two fingers to touch on the pubic bone of the recipient. Howard had glimpsed the photos for that set of touch points in the training manual one day, and wasn't pleased with the idea of his wife touching a man that way. So, did I promise my husband that I would never include a lower abdominal set when working on a male recipient? Yes, I did. But would I ever perform a lower abdominal set on a man if it was an emergency? You bet I would.

Feeling grateful for all I had learned, I basked in the glory of my accomplishment, while ignoring any doubts or concerns. I knew there might be some challenges facing me as a certified practitioner at the center. But I was confident that I could handle whatever was coming my way. After all, how bad could it get?

CHAPTER FIVE

New Lessons to Learn

There's no hurt so great that love can't heal it.

—Richard Paul Evans

The Gift

Now that I was certified, I could escape the scrutiny I had been under by other certified practitioners at the center. Confident in my knowledge, I savored the freedom of working on people alone. The icing on the cake, though, was how delightful it was getting to know my recipients. There was a steady stream of new ones to work on, as well as my regulars—those who had standing appointments with me every week. During sessions, they'd share colorful stories about their lives. Often they were curious to hear about my life, as well.

Too bad I wasn't yet adept at carrying on a conversation and touching the precise points at the same time. There I would be, happily chatting with a recipient, when I would realize how far off the mark my fingers had drifted. With a quiet gasp, I would make the necessary corrections, relieved that the recipient didn't seem to notice. At least for the time being, I needed to yak less and focus on my recipients more.

Lisa, a young woman with a high-pressure job, sighed a few times as I touched her stress points. One of my favorite things was hearing tense, uptight recipients sigh like that. It indicated that they were beginning to relax. I would sigh right along with them. I wasn't sure why that happened, but it felt great for me to unwind, too. As I touched around Lisa's shoulders, she fell asleep. She snored, her lips making little puffing sounds. Suddenly, she sagged forward as if bending in half. I was scared she'd tumble headfirst off the table, so I pulled back on her upper arms, jolting her awake.

"Wha . . . oh, I'm sorry. I guess I'm a little sleep-deprived," she muttered.

"A little?" I challenged. "You're so tired, I think you'd have hit the floor and kept on sleeping."

Soledad was one of my regular recipients. One day she couldn't wait to show me how much better she was feeling. Wearing a radiant smile, she hopped on the massage table and lifted up her arms. Then she wiggled her thumbs, laughing as my eyes grew wide with amazement. When I first started working on her, only a few months before, arthritis pain flared from her hands to her shoulders. Her arm mobility was severely limited; her thumbs were almost frozen in place. As I watched her hands dance, tears sprang to my eyes. My heart expanded and filled my chest with fluttery feelings. I was embarrassed to be crying, but Soledad didn't care that my mascara was running like a dark river down my face. She just hugged me.

Annie, a middle-aged woman who suffered with back pain, possessed strength and courage that was awe-inspiring. She revealed that she'd been sexually abused as a teenager, and still couldn't tolerate being touched in most situations. But she forced herself to accept my fingers as they moved over her body.

"I can't believe how safe Bio-Touch makes me feel," she said, smiling through her tears. "I never thought I would ever again be able to relax with someone's hands on me."

Of course her tears triggered the flow of my own. During practitioner training, we'd been taught that sometimes during a session, recipients opened up about things they'd suffered in the past. We were told not to be concerned if they began to cry while working through their painful issues. We were to continue the session, knowing they'd feel better after the emotional cleansing. I just wished I knew how to prevent myself from crying along with them.

Another time, Edwin, a middle-aged man who had suffered a stroke years before, told me he could tell his weak side was getting stronger after months of regular sessions. "All the practitioners here have helped me a lot, but I think I improve even faster after each session with you," he said.

I appreciated his kind words. But I was deeply touched by observing his increased level of mobility, and the realization that I had been among those helping him achieve it. Before, he'd needed his walker to get any-where. Now, the walker stayed by the couch as Edwin took sturdy steps, unaided, to a session room—a distance of nearly forty feet. And once on the massage table, he could turn himself over with greater ease.

Angela, a quiet, sad-looking young woman, was not only a new recipient of mine, but a first-time recipient to the center, as well. After leading her to a session room, I explained the basic information given to all newcomers. Then I asked her to fill out a form detailing painful areas or conditions that she wanted me to address. When I saw she had written "a broken heart" on the form, I was speechless . . . something that rarely happened to me. I left her alone to undress while I washed my hands. Paul was standing by the sink.

"I have a new recipient who wrote "broken heart" on the form," I said.

"Okay," he answered.

"Well, what should I do for her?"

"What do you mean?" he asked.

"I mean what set of points should I perform on her for a broken heart? It isn't a physical condition. It's emotional," I pointed out.

"That doesn't matter," he answered. "Just perform the set of points that we touch when addressing the heart. You know that Bio-Touch helps everyone feel emotionally nurtured. Her heart hurts. Touching around it will help ease her pain whether it's from a physical or emo-tional cause."

"Oh, okay. That does make sense when you put it like that."

Angela sat as rigid as a monument when I first touched her, but soon her hands unclenched and her tense shoulders dropped into a relaxed position. She offered very little in the way of conversation, so I worked in silence. She returned a few times over the next several weeks, looking a bit more cheerful with each visit. Sometimes she even smiled. Angela never explained what or who had broken her heart. I was curi-ous, but it wasn't my place to ask. Over those weeks she had gained some inner strength, and that was good enough for me.

Several months later, a second recipient came to me with a bro-ken heart. Kathy was grieving because her beloved cat had passed away. When she described the amazing bond she had had with her pet, I felt that familiar lump rising in my throat. But I got busy touching around her heart, hoping my focus would stifle my tears. It worked. I was delighted to see Kathy's nerve-wracked body unwind, giving her the break she needed from the stress of mourning.

Sometimes while giving a session, it was as hard to contain my laughter as my tears. I had to bite my lip to keep from chuckling aloud. Meg, a spry lady in her late seventies, told me she was happy her back no longer hurt since I had worked on it several times.

"But now," she said in a softer voice, "I need you to concentrate right here." She pointed to her lower abdomen. "I sleep with my dog, and lately at night, my intestinal gas escapes so loudly, it sounds like a machine gun. It wakes me up and scares Jingo so bad, he runs out of the room!"

Caroline, a woman in her eighties, came in for her third appointment with me. She grasped my hands in hers as I finished working on her knees.

"I really appreciate your volunteering to help people like me. Thanks to you, my knees are so much stronger now, and I have so much less pain," she said, eyes aglow. "But the best thing is . . . I smell like me, again."

"You smell like you?" I asked, confused.

"I do . . . because I don't have to rub in that stinky sports cream anymore. That stuff didn't help anyway." She waved her hand with disgust. "Now, instead of smelling like my arthritic brother-in-law, I smell like Jean Naté. I have her entire line of products."

As gratifying as it was to be part of such meaningful and amusing experiences, volunteering at the center wasn't all roses for me. While I enjoyed working on knees, backs, arms, hands, legs, heads and necks, I struggled when I had to work on feet. I hated feet. Even as a child I regarded them as ugly, neglected things that peeked grotesquely out of sandals. Naked and vulnerable, they were often displayed for the world to see, when they should have been hiding inside socks and shoes.

I think my loathing of feet started the day I had a play date at my friend Carolyn's house. I was six years old. We were sitting on her living room carpet playing the board game *Sorry*. Carolyn's mom, a pretty woman, kicked off the beautiful black and white peep-toe high heels she was wearing. Then she sat on the couch, rolling down her stockings. My eyes shifted to the woman's feet as she rubbed them. I stared in horror. The skin was flaky and mottled with blue and purple veins that clashed with her blood-red nail polish. Several misshapen toes sported thick, yellowed corns. Knobby bumps protruded from her insteps. I turned away with a stomachache, wishing she'd put her shoes back on. It was fitting that we were playing *Sorry*. I sure was sorry I'd seen that woman's feet.

My own toes weren't gorgeous, but I always made sure they were lotioned and pedicured or covered up. Our daughter, Jill, actually had the prettiest feet I had ever seen, while our son David's wide flippers always made me smile. And although Howard's feet were decent-looking, I hadn't offered him a foot massage in nearly four decades of marriage.

But now, people were looking to me to ease their throbbing, aching hooves. I was expected to touch their cracked, crusty heels, sweat-sticky soles, fungus-covered nails, and hairy toes—all in various stages of cleanliness. Ugh. Each one of those things, alone, grossed me out, but seeing them in assorted combinations made me gag every time.

With gritted teeth I approached feet like they were stink bombs with a hair trigger. What saved me was that I only had to touch them with the tips of my fingers. So, I could act like things were normal—even carry on a conversation—while my guts privately roiled. If I had needed to make full palm contact, or massage down between toes, I would have been a goner.

Aside from feet, I was feeling pretty satisfied with my growing level of competency at the center. Nothing had popped up that I couldn't handle. Maybe I was a bit too cocky, though, because just when I was riding high, an incident knocked me right out of the saddle.

A recipient, whom I shall refer to as Ms. X, showed up for her first appointment with me. On her chart, I could see that her initial appointment had been a week before. Tod had worked on her. No specific complaints were noted, other than stress and a mild cough.

After I introduced myself to the woman, who looked to be about my age, I led her to a session room. I asked her to take her shirt off, saying I would be back after washing my hands. I also asked her permission to have an intern work with me. She agreed.

Serena had been an intern for only a short time, and I was thrilled to be in the position to show someone else the ropes for a change. We washed our hands, then knocked on the session room door.

"Come in," the recipient called out in a pleasant tone.

As we entered the room, the sight of Ms. X sitting stark naked on the table greeted us. But instead of looking vulnerable or exposed, she looked formidable. Her head was held high, her shoulders pulled back. I shot a quick glance at Serena, whose stunned expression matched my own.

"I am so sorry," I gasped. "You must have misunderstood me. You only needed to remove your shirt. Let me get something to cover you with."

"Oh, I heard you. I prefer to be nude," she announced. Her expression was one of defiance.

There were a number of women I gave regular sessions to who never wore bras. I had finally gotten used to that, though it took a while. But sitting before me now was a nude, middle-aged woman with a body typical of a non-athlete of that age. And she seemed as comfortable as a supermodel posing on a beach.

"Well okay, let's start your session," I said, forcing my eyebrows back down from the middle of my forehead. Shaking, I reached under the table for a clean sheet to drape around the woman's lower half while Serena began touching the "greeting points" on her solar plexus and neck area.

Ms. X smiled. "I don't need that around me," she said, flinging the sheet away with the back of her hand. It drifted to the floor, coming to rest next to my feet. She stretched out on the table, opened her legs, and pointed to a place where her pubic area and the inside of her upper thigh met. "Here's where it hurts. Touch here," she ordered.

My nostrils prickled at the unpleasant odor that exuded from her. I bent down to pick up the discarded sheet, quickly covering her again. Serena and I exchanged wide-eyed looks from opposite sides of the table.

"How long have you been experiencing the pain?" I asked Ms. X in my most polite voice.

Her tongue tsked with impatience. "Oh, I don't know . . . it comes and goes."

"Did you suffer an injury?" I persisted.

"Not that I remember. It just hurts, okay? It hurts right here." She kicked at the sheet sending it back to the floor. Then, with her eyes on mine, she patted the area in question with her index finger.

My bowels tightened. The spot she pointed to was located in a place that I wouldn't have touched for a million dollars. After seeing the expression on my face, Serena buried her face in her hands, her shoulders quaking with suppressed laughter.

"Let's keep this around you for our comfort as well as yours," I suggested, grabbing a second fresh sheet from under the table. I covered Ms. X again, leaving the first sheet where it was—balled up on the floor. Then I began to touch around her outer thigh.

"That's not the right spot," she snapped. She grabbed the new sheet, whipping it off before I could react. It briefly clung to the side of the table as if for dear life, before joining the first one on the carpeting below. "Touch right here."

Her finger zeroed in, again, on the now well-established area. She glowered at me while slowly shaking her head. Then sighing, she spread her legs, again, stretching her arms over her head.

Serena pressed her lips together so hard they turned white. Anger blazed through me. I had enough of Ms. X's rude demands, and the way she was trying to bully me—especially in front of an intern. And although I wasn't sure what she wanted from me, I knew I had to take command of the situation.

"Actually," I said sounding calmer than I felt, "we don't need to touch on the exact point of the pain. As long as we're in the general vicinity— even two or three inches away—we're still going to get good results."

It was a true statement. But even if it wasn't, I would have said it anyway. Ms. X's dubious expression told me she wasn't buying it. I didn't care. I bent over and picked up both sheets from the floor, stubbornly re-wrapping the woman. Serena figured out a way to hold the ends of the sheets together, keeping our recipient inside our makeshift straitjacket. For the rest of the session, I strategically uncovered her as I needed to.

After her session, Ms. X dressed rapidly, walking out of the center without speaking to anyone, or making another appointment. Serena and I hurried to the sink, soaping our hands for a long time without saying a word. But once we dared to make eye contact, snorts of pent-up laughter burst from our lips.

"You handled that situation really well," Serena said. "You were so calm and cool about it."

"Well thank you, but it was all an act," I admitted. "On the inside I was screaming the whole time."

We cleaned and disinfected the room. As Serena covered the table with fresh sheets, I gathered up all the dirty ones, carrying them as far from my body as my arms would allow. As I stuffed them into the washing machine, Paul appeared on the patio. I jumped at the opportunity to tell him what had happened.

"That's incredible," he said with a perplexed look on his face. "Last week Tod told me she was one of the most difficult people he'd ever worked on. But he didn't mention that she'd been inappropriate. I've never heard of anyone demanding to be touched like that before."

"Just my luck it would happen to me," I complained.

"Luck had nothing to do with it, Debra. It happened to you for the same reason you always get the recipients that need their feet worked on," Paul said, a grin spreading across his face. "Those challenges are learning experiences the universe designed especially for you."

"But, why do I have to have them?"

"They're to help you become free from judgments, fears, and pre-conceived notions about yourself and others, so you can know what you're capable of, and grow in your own self-awareness."

"Well, I don't think I freed myself from judgments in that session room just now," I said, shaking my head. "If anything, I may have become more judgmental. But even though I wanted to slap the rudeness right out of her, I controlled myself. I didn't know I could handle something like that."

Paul nodded. "See how much you've learned already?"

A few months later, though, the universe sent a challenge designed to test me to the core. I'll call this recipient Jake. It was Jake's first time at the center, so I welcomed him, leading the nice-looking, thirty-something-year-old man to a session room. After I explained the process, he filled out the paperwork, indicating he was seeking help with a skin condition called psoriasis. Thinking nothing of it, I asked him to remove his sweatshirt while I went to wash my hands.

When I re-entered the room, my heart dropped to my stomach. I fought the urge to turn around and run out the door. The skin on Jake's chest, abdomen, and back was awash with angry, scaly, red patches. Many areas were so raw and inflamed, they looked like thick slices of corned beef.

I had never seen, let alone touched, anyone with such a severe skin condition. Its disfiguring ability was shocking. I inhaled deeply, desperately trying to remember anything I ever heard about psoriasis. I didn't even know if it was contagious. I just knew I didn't want to touch this young man with my bare hands.

I faked a smile, making small talk to conceal my agitation. My voice sounded as breathy as a marathon runner's. All the saliva evaporated from my mouth. My pulse thumped in my ears as I touched only the areas of his skin that were healthy looking.

But when my fingers accidently brushed a scab, I felt chills racing up my back. I shuddered, wishing I could plunge my hands into some Clorox. I considered telling the young man that I was ill, and had to leave, but I wasn't sure I could be convincing. I didn't want to hurt his feelings. As I stalled for time, I placed my fingertips on some safe areas around his neck.

Then I remembered how we'd been taught in our classes that our comfort was as important as our recipient's. But I didn't know if that absolved me in this case. I wasn't sure if I was merely uncomfortable touching someone who looked like that, or whether I was rightfully, sensibly scared of catching his affliction. It was a defining moment, but I only had seconds to make the decision.

My gut told me that if I truly wanted to help people, this was part of the deal. So holding my breath, I moved my fingers to his back, trying to avoid the worst areas. When that wasn't possible, I gritted my teeth to keep my revulsion and fear under control.

"I'm sorry . . . is it okay if my—um—my fingers get close to the areas of psoriasis?" I had to ask; I prayed he'd say no.

"Oh, yes. It's fine. No problem at all," Jake answered, in an upbeat tone.

My heart sank; I was stuck. I needed to know if psoriasis was contagious, but I just couldn't force the words out. I thought of all the commercials I had seen on television for the condition. Of course, they never showed what it really looked like or explained whether it could spread to another. They merely spoke about the misery and embarrassment of it. Now I understood why.

My stomach clenched as I felt those crusty edges of his skin. I forced myself to endure what had to be the longest session I ever gave. My feelings alternated from compassion for him, to guilt for wanting to run away from him.

After the session, Jake met me at the front desk. He wanted another appointment with me for the following Friday. I smiled as I handed him a date reminder card, my lips frozen in place. After he left, I ran to the bathroom. I had already washed my hands four times while Jake was getting his shirt back on. But I itched to scrub them again. Rifling through the various cleaners in the cabinet under the sink, I grabbed the scouring powder, sprinkling it over my hands. I rinsed with water as hot as I could stand. Then for good measure, I sprayed glass cleaner, watching the blue liquid bubble through my fingers.

I stared at myself in the mirror; I looked as scared as I felt. Damn it, how come no one else struggled like I did? All the other certified practitioners seemed to handle their recipients with ease. I was in over my head. Obviously I wasn't cut out for this kind of service.

My shift was over for the day, so I slipped out the back door, unnoticed. There was a lump in my throat, and I knew if someone looked at me, I'd burst into tears. As I drove home, I obsessed about Jake. Of course the first thing I did when I walked through the door was jump on the computer to research psoriasis. It was a great relief to learn that it wasn't contagious, but I was still upset. I told Howard the whole story as we ate dinner.

"You touched someone with your bare hands when you weren't sure if his condition was contagious or not?" His tone was soft, but he looked like he'd just heard the stupidest thing, ever.

Propping my elbows on the table, I cupped my chin in my hands. "Yes, I did."

"I appreciate your dedication, but please," Howard insisted, "the next time you're in a situation like that, find out if it's contagious. It's only fair to you . . . and to me, too. We both could have been exposed to something dangerous."

I pushed my plate away. "You're right, honey. It was a risky thing to do. But I didn't think I had a choice. Meanwhile, he's coming back next week, and I don't want to touch his skin—contagious or not."

"Didn't you ask Paul about all this . . . to find out what to do?"

"No. I just couldn't talk about it."

"Well, you better call him tonight," Howard said. "This is an important issue that obviously didn't come up in training class. You need to know how to handle it."

"Okay, I will."

But I didn't call Paul. Instead, I marinated in my own misery, questioning whether I had the conviction to move forward on this path I had started down. I felt like a phony. I had looked forward to helping people heal for so long. But now I dreaded going back to the center; I dreaded touching a man who really needed my help.

I couldn't get the images of Jake's skin out of my mind. I pictured my own skin looking like that, and it terrified me. If I ever came down with a similar condition, I would hide from the world, but how could I hide from my husband or myself?

I knew Howard loved me more than anything, but if my skin suddenly looked like Jake's, how repelled would he be? Would he look away? Would he cringe when he touched me? Would he want to leave me? Could I blame him? Fears and insecurities I didn't even know I had, flooded my mind. Wrapping myself in a soft blanket, I slumped in my favorite chair, playing Mozart's *Requiem* repeatedly. The haunting tones matched my mood to perfection.

I knew I had to call Paul before my upcoming shift on Friday, but I dreaded the thought. I was embarrassed to admit my true feelings. I didn't want him to find out that I was the most superficial certified practitioner he'd ever worked with. And I was concerned he'd doubt my capacity to love thy neighbor as thyself, the guiding principle of Bio-Touch.

"Ah, another test for Debra!" he exclaimed on Thursday night when I finally called him. I had admitted the truth about everything. I even told him my fears about contracting a disfiguring disease.

"You're really being challenged here," he continued. "The first thing is, you never have to touch someone if you're not comfortable doing so. More importantly, you never touch someone if their condition is contagious. If a recipient comes to the center with shingles, we never touch directly on the lesions because the condition is so contagious. I'm sorry if that wasn't made clearer in class. It's perfectly acceptable to ask a recipient if they're contagious or not. They should understand your concerns. Or you can excuse yourself and come find me or another certified practitioner to ask if you're in doubt. Either way, just relax, okay? You're experiencing some unique situations here, and you're doing fine with them."

"Well, that's a relief," I sighed.

"Now, as far as not wanting to touch Jake again, there's only one way to think about that."

"And what's that?" I pleaded.

"Think of it as just another challenging part of your journey—through Bio-Touch—to conquer your pre-conceived judgments and fears. And those fears run deep. So deep, they even have you questioning your husband's love—if you should ever develop a deforming disease," Paul continued. "You need to talk to Howard. Tell him your fears of his rejection if you should ever lose your health or attractiveness. He'll help shine the light of truth and love on those fears, and you'll see they're not rational. They'll melt away, and your capacity for growth and self-awareness will be impossible to measure."

"Maybe I can't handle any more challenges, or being more self-aware," I grumbled. "Maybe my judgments and fears are best left hidden in the dark."

"I promise you this. Once you accept your challenges with love . . . once you really open your heart to them, they'll disappear."

"What? Are you saying that if I open my heart to Jake, the fear and the challenge will disappear?"

"Yes it will, because you'll have overcome that challenge by learning your own capacity to love. It was no accident that Jake showed up as your recipient. He's here to teach you."

When we hung up, my head was spinning. Paul had spoken of things I couldn't comprehend. But in the meantime, I decided to take his advice and share my fears with Howard. After taking a deep breath, I sat down next to my husband as he read a book on the couch.

Feeling my eyes on him, he looked up from the page. "What's up?" he asked.

"What would happen if I came down with something like psoriasis?" I blurted out.

He looked puzzled. "What do you mean what would happen? We'd deal with it. It'd be alright."

"But you're easily grossed out," I persisted. "Wouldn't you be repulsed by me? Wouldn't you want to leave me—you know, trade me in for a newer model?" I tried to make a joke, but my voice cracked, betraying me.

Howard's chocolate eyes searched my face. Then he smiled his most impish grin. "Well, I might be a little grossed out, sure. But no, I wouldn't leave . . . even if you got an icky skin disease or all your teeth fell out. I love you. I would never leave you. I think you know that by now, don't you?"

I felt so ashamed; how could I have forgotten? He'd proven that to me years before. I had just turned forty, and after following advice that women that age should perform a breast self-exam, I found a small lump. I was shocked, then devastated at my healthy body's betrayal. Thank heavens it turned out to be nothing serious, and didn't require treatment. But it took longer than a week before that was confirmed by a needle biopsy. During that difficult waiting period, Howard was with me constantly, loving and supportive. I remember warning him that if I needed surgery, I would be left with a scar. I needed to know how he'd feel if one of his favorite body parts was marred.

He had held my hand, and said, "If you have a scar, I'll kiss it every day."

And in the glow of that poignant memory, I snuggled into my husband's strong embrace. "Thank you, Howard, for reminding me how lucky I am."

Later, I drifted off to sleep after praying for the strength to deal with Jake. Nevertheless, when I arrived at the center the next day, I was filled with apprehension. The young man arrived early for his appointment. He sat leafing through a magazine while I said goodbye to another recipient.

Forcing a smile to my lips, I led Jake to a session room. I reminded him to remove his shirt, and said I'd be right back. As I washed up, I stared at my defeated-looking face in the mirror. Then I remembered Paul's words. I had to give love to my challenge so it would go away. I closed my eyes and concentrated. I conjured up the image of arms of golden light reaching out from my heart to embrace Jake. The vision shimmered, dazzling my inner eye. Yes, it was exquisite, but how could it make my problem disappear?

Making my way to the session room, I dragged my feet like a prisoner walking the last mile to the electric chair. I was nervous to see what state Jake's psoriasis would be in. If it was still bad, could I handle it? Would I be able to rise above myself and concentrate on him?

Holding my breath, I opened the door. Thank heavens, even in the low light of the room, I could see that the redness and swelling of his skin had eased considerably. What a world of difference from the previous week. Still, I was reluctant to touch him.

But this time, my stomach didn't clench when my fingers brushed over a scabby or scaly area. In fact, I felt fine. Touching Jake's skin was no big deal. I could handle it! That was such an astonishing revelation, I was sorry I couldn't share my excitement with him. And with all the celebratory noise going on inside my head, I almost missed what he was saying.

"As you can see, Bio-Touch really helped the flare-up I had last week. I wasn't sure it would, with all the stress I've been under lately."

"Oh? What's so stressful in your life, Jake, if you don't mind my asking?"

"Well I'm moving to Connecticut on Tuesday, so there are a lot of things I have to get done."

"You're . . . you're moving?" Somehow, I managed to speak over the choir singing the "Hallelujah Chorus" in my head.

"Yes. I've been interviewing, and I landed a new job."

"What wonderful news," I said, with a deeper sincerity than he could have imagined. "I wish you all the best in your new endeavor."

"Thank you." His smile was radiant.

"Does anyone else at the center know you're moving, Jake? Did you happen to mention it to Paul?"

"No, you're the only one I told. Why?"

"Oh, no reason," I said, chuckling to myself.

After I hugged Jake goodbye, I sighed with relief. Then I ran to tell Paul about my conjured golden image of love for Jake, and how he was moving across the country.

"See?" Paul's face glowed. "You gave love to your challenge, and now it's going away. It always does."

"How does that work, again? I don't get it," I persisted, wishing I'd known about this life-changer years ago.

"Well, whatever is within us is what we project outward," he answered. "We live in either fear or love. Fear projects separation, judgments, and problems. Love is the realization that we are all truly connected to everyone else. When we love—truly love—it erases our fears so we're left with only our purity to project. It's like magic. And it's the main reason I practice Bio-Touch."

I smiled and nodded, although I didn't understand most of what he was talking about. All I knew for sure was how he'd been right about giving love to my challenge. I yearned for the kind of insight and knowledge he possessed. I just hoped he hadn't acquired it solely by meditating for hours on end.

When mid-December rolled around, it was time for the center's annual holiday party thrown for all the practitioners and recipients, spouses, and friends. Everyone brought food for the scrumptious potluck dinner that included appetizers, entrees, salads, side dishes, and delectable desserts. A "stealing" gift exchange provided plenty of laughter.

After the festivities, there was a small awards ceremony. Paul bestowed the Volunteer of the Year certificate upon Janice, a certified practitioner and instructor chosen for her outstanding spirit and dedication. Janice stood to accept her award to warm applause.

The Self-Awareness Award was the other certificate to be given out. It emphasized how growing in one's self-awareness was one of the fundamental elements of sharing Bio-Touch. That award was given to me.

Everyone agreed that I was the certified practitioner who had traveled farthest on that road in the year 2010.

So it was with deep pride that I stood and accepted the award when Paul announced my name. As everyone applauded, I looked around thinking how far I had come since first setting foot inside the Bio-Touch Center fourteen months earlier. Back then, I worried about joining some strange people who were promoting a healing technique that seemed too good to be true.

Now I felt honored to be among them. I had already learned so much about myself within the Center's environment of acceptance. And I was using my hands to make people feel better—something I had wanted to do for so many years. My eyes rested on Howard, who smiled and clapped for my achievement. Joy swelled within me as I realized how all the pieces of my life were melding perfectly together.

Defeating the Darkness

*In everyone's life, at some time, our inner fire goes out. It is then
burst into flame by an encounter with another human being. We
should all be thankful for those people who rekindle the inner spirit.*

Albert Schweitzer
Out of My Life and Thought

A few months after the holiday party, Paul and I sat on opposite sides
of the reception desk waiting for our next recipients to arrive. With no
one else around, it was a rare, quiet moment at the center.

"Recipients have asked me over the years whether they can develop
a dependency on Bio-Touch," Paul said.

"Oh? Well, I never thought of that," I admitted. "Can they?"

"No more than they could become dependent on brushing their
teeth, eating a healthy diet, or any other preventative habit. It's not possible to become physically dependent on Bio-Touch, but it's so good at
maintaining health, everyone should regularly receive it."

"I guess that makes sense," I nodded.

"But," Paul mused, "I've also been asked—and wondered myself—
what would happen if people received regular Bio-Touch sessions from
birth to old age? I would love to see the results of that experiment, to
see how healthy and pain-free those elderly folks would be."

I smiled, imagining newborn babies on our massage tables in
assembly-line fashion, while spry elders did the tango in the waiting
room. "What other interesting questions have you been asked over the
years?" I ventured.

"Well, the one I'm probably asked the most is: 'How can a simple
healing method be so effective at reducing pain and stress?' And as
you know, we don't really know," Paul said, becoming animated. "It's

65

so simple, all you need are fingers—and you don't even need many of those. I once taught Bio-Touch to a woman in Hawaii who'd suffered severe disfigurement due to leprosy. The disease left her with only a couple of fingers, but she was still as effective at using the technique as anybody I'd ever seen!"

"Wow, that's amazing," I said. Even though I had come a long way in the area of self-awareness, I knew I wasn't ready to work on someone with leprosy. I silently prayed I wouldn't receive that challenge anytime soon.

"Also," Paul continued, "people ask what makes Bio-Touch different from other healing touch techniques. They want to know what makes it so special."

"And what do you say?"

"I say it's magical the way Bio-Touch reaches down to that scared child in all of us and promotes feelings of well-being and love. Bio-Touch is love. Love is Bio-Touch. It's all we do here—we give people love. We're not here to fix people, but to serve them. We get to participate in their healing, and feel their joy. It empowers people to help other people. And if those people just happen to heal in the process? Perfect."

A warm feeling spread through me. "That's a great way to think of it."

"Another question people ask is why we don't charge for our services here at the center," Paul said, leaning his elbows on the desktop and interlacing his fingers. "They caution me about the value of something becoming underrated when it's simply given away."

"So, what's your answer? Why don't we charge?"

Paul smiled, his cobalt eyes glistening in their sockets. "Because we can't charge people for the truth."

I stared at him. "Whoa. What does that mean, exactly?"

"There's one truth that resides within each of us," he answered. "It is our birthright. No one can charge us to obtain that truth—it's already ours. Bio-Touch is like truth. Our capacity to heal is within each of us. We have a birthright to be happy and healthy. So, how can we charge for that? Over the years, I've noticed that many people seem to instinctively 'know' Bio-Touch on some level, once they start giving or receiving it. Our only job is to give them the tools to reawaken what they already know."

We sat in silence for a few moments as I digested his words.

"And one more question I get a lot," he continued, "is about how I envision the future of Bio-Touch. That's easy. I see everyone on the planet eventually having access to our classes or being able to download the training manual from our website. That way, even in the most remote homes of Bangladesh or China, people could share Bio-Touch with their family and friends. Everyone would feel better. Actually, a book needs to be written about Bio-Touch. A book could introduce it to people everywhere."

A sudden jolt of electricity snaked through me. My mind screamed that I should write that book. The idea thrilled me, but self-doubt slapped me back to reality. "Paul," I asked, "Did I ever tell you that my daughter, Jill, is a writer as well as the editor-in-chief of a magazine?"

"Yes. I remember you showed me some of her articles. Are you suggesting she might be interested in writing the Bio-Touch book?"

"It's possible," I answered with a shrug. "Her job keeps her pretty busy, though."

"That's okay," he said, "She can take her time with it. I've wished for someone to write this book for over twenty years. I know how to be patient."

"But, if a Bio-Touch book is written and people around the world learn about it, then what?" I asked, handing him Jill's business card.

"Then," Paul said, taking a deep breath, "I'll be able to close these doors and retire." He raised his index finger. "However, the doors will remain open for as long as even one person needs to come in for a session."

And with that, he jumped up from his chair to welcome his next recipient, who was walking through the front door. He smiled at the man as he led him to a session room.

I trembled with excitement. Even though I mentioned Jill because of her professional background, in my head I saw myself writing the Bio-Touch book. The problem was, I hadn't written professionally; I'd only created stories for my own enjoyment. Sure, I won writing contests in school, but that was decades ago. I didn't know if I even possessed the skills and obsession necessary to write a book. So I decided to keep quiet about it.

"Mom, Paul called me," Jill said over the phone, a few days later. "I'm sure a Bio-Touch book would help a lot of people, but I really don't have time to work on such a big project right now. I've been thinking, though, that you should be the one to write it. What do you say?"

My jaw dropped. "What do I say?" A tingling sensation spread through my body; my feet started moving like an Irish River Dancer. "I say that's fantastic because I've been dying to write it!"

"Then, you should go for it, Mom," Jill insisted. "You've got the time, and you've certainly got the passion for the subject. You've always been my writing mentor, so I know you'll do a great job. You've talked about writing a book someday. Well, someday has arrived."

"Thank you, so much, for your faith in me, sweetheart!"

A few days later, Jill was in town for a weekend visit. I drove her to the Bio-Touch Center, so she could give Paul a face-to-face answer about writing the book. I was nervous as we settled ourselves around a small table.

Jill began the conversation by apologizing. "I'm so sorry, Paul, but I won't be able to take on the project of writing the book. I'm just too busy at work right now.

"That's okay, I understand," he replied, hiding any emotion he might have felt.

"However," Jill said, a smile playing on her lips, "I happen to know someone who would love to write the book, and would do a great job."

"Really? Who?" Paul asked.

Jill shifted her eyes to meet mine, her hand gesturing toward me. Paul's eyes followed. It took him a moment to understand. Then, a look of surprise came over his face.

"You?"

"Yes, me," I answered. "I write a little . . . for fun. I'd really love to write the Bio-Touch book." Searching his face for signs of disappointment, I was relieved that I didn't see any.

"Well, that's great," he said with a laugh. "In fact, it's perfect."

Two weeks later Paul visited my home for the first of many weekly interviews. As he breezed through my door, he said he hadn't realized how close we lived to each other. We laughed at the coincidence that our homes were not only on the same side of Tucson, but were only three miles apart.

We settled into the den where I armed myself with a digital voice recorder, pads of legal paper, and pens. I was anxious to capture the history of Bio-Touch, as well as examine the pivotal role Paul played in its growth. He was, after all, the one who recognized Bio-Touch's potential, expanded it beyond the confines of a healer's house in Colorado, and shared it for years in various locations. Plus, I continued to be curious about Paul's past. I wanted to know how he'd obtained his deep spiritual knowledge, and hear what influenced him toward a lifetime of service to others.

"Paul, the philosophy 'love thy neighbor as thyself' obviously has special meaning for you," I said, trying to sound professional. "When did that principle first surface in your life?"

"I'd say it began when I closed my eyes and made a wish as I blew out the candles on my birthday cake," he answered. "I was five years old, and I remember wishing that everyone in the world could be happy. I wasn't very happy with my wish, though. I wondered why I couldn't have wished for a bicycle, or something normal like the other kids in the neighborhood would have. But I was already aware of how different I was from them."

"Well, besides that unusual wish, how else were you different from the other kids?" I asked.

"Oh, I was the weird one who never wanted to have punching matches or play-fights with any of them. I just didn't want to hurt anybody. The father of one of the kids even tried to teach me how to fight a few times," he said, shaking his head at the memory. "But my heart wasn't in it, so I just shrugged my shoulders and walked away."

"Yep, you were definitely not the average kid. So, what was your family life like?"

"It was good. I was raised in a nice house in an upscale neighborhood outside of Los Angeles, California. My father, Carl, was a businessman, who loved his family and always wanted the best for us, even if it meant going into debt. He was good at hiding the fact that he overspent and was supporting us on credit. My mother was a loving, beautiful, involved, stay-at-home mom, who was devoted to her family. My brother, Bruce, was two years younger than me. We were a close, loving family."

"Sounds like a happy childhood. Did that continue as you grew older?"

"Yes. I enjoyed school, earned good grades, and played sports. But even then, I had a gnawing desire to help others. One way I did that was by joining the student council. There, I began to speak my mind on

various school issues that were important to me and other sixth grad-
ers. We strove to create changes for the better."

"What else was significant at that time of your life?"

"I began to seek answers about my Jewish faith, wanting to understand more about God's laws and God's love. My parents were spiritual
people, but not particularly religious, and didn't attend Temple regularly. So, I began walking to Temple by myself every Friday night and
Saturday morning to attend Sabbath services. The importance of the
Golden Rule—treating others as you'd like to be treated—really became
clear to me there."

"You voluntarily went to Temple by yourself?" I asked.

"Yes. I enjoyed it. My parents weren't even surprised, because I often
did my own things, alone. And I spent every summer at Camp Scotmar,
an overnight camp located outside of Los Angeles, where I eventually
became a senior counselor. I had fun working with the children, but I
really loved helping them learn to find solutions to their problems. It
was the perfect summer job. Eventually, though, the camp moved its
operations to Colorado."

"When and where did you go to college? And what did you study?"

"I entered San Diego State University as a freshman in 1969, major-
ing in mathematics. I thought I'd enjoy a career teaching arithmetic
to children. Along with my required classes, I took classes in wom-
en's studies, Chicano studies, and African-American literature, which
opened my eyes to the suffering of so many people around the world. I
began to realize how sheltered my friends and I'd been growing up in
our comfortable lives . . . receiving new cars for our sixteenth birthdays,
and never wanting for anything."

"So you earned a degree in mathematics?"

"No, I actually changed majors because of a nightmare. I dreamed I
was standing in front of a chalkboard in a classroom full of kids. I was
wearing black, over-sized glasses, and a stiff, uncomfortable shirt and tie.
I was miserable trying to teach math to rows of bored, unruly kids. They
refused to listen, turning their backs and laughing. I woke up sweating.
Weeks later, I still couldn't shake the feeling that it was a warning."

"Ha, sounds like it," I agreed.

"So, I decided to take a career placement test. The results showed
that I would excel as a preacher, counselor, or youth program director.

So, I immediately changed my major to a newly-offered program called Recreation Administration. I knew I'd never earn much money in that kind of career, but making lots of money was never important to me."

"So, changing your field of study was a good move for you, then?" I asked, scribbling on my legal pad in case the voice recorder wasn't working.

"Yes, it was a much better option for me. So, I just started my sophomore year, happily settling into my new classes. Then the bomb dropped."

"Bomb? What bomb?"

"My parents called to inform me that they were getting divorced. Apparently, they grew apart. My dad fell in love with another woman, and was moving to a different city to be with her."

"And you had no idea? It was out of the blue?"

"It was completely out of the blue for me, at least. I was shocked. I remember feeling my stomach churn as I listened to my parents attempt to explain it. I couldn't listen anymore, so I made an excuse to get off the phone. After I hung up I stared into space for a long time, trying to wrap my mind around it all."

"That must have been tough to deal with," I said.

"I tried to shrug it off, telling myself that it was no big deal. Hey, I'd be just another typical white, middle-class college kid with divorced parents. So what? I figured my future was still bright. I wouldn't be affected too much by their break up. I'd be just fine. But soon, I felt sadness unlike anything I'd ever known before. I just wasn't able to experience joy at all."

"Sounds like you were depressed," I frowned, stating the obvious.

"Yeah, the smallest things made me cry, which was inconvenient as well as embarrassing. So, I spent more and more time alone. Meals held little interest for me—even my favorite foods didn't smell or taste right. But sleep became my best friend; I could escape into the blackness and forget everything for hours."

"You needed help. Wasn't there anyone to turn to?"

"Well, I drove home to Los Angeles quite often to visit my mother and brother, as well as my girlfriend, Lauren, whom I'd gone steady with since high school. I thought seeing them would lift my spirits, but the blackness continued. I was home, but things seemed unfamiliar and weird without my dad there. Finally, when I couldn't stop crying, my mom called our family doctor who gave me tranquilizer shots and prescribed tranquilizer pills to take back to school with me. The drugs didn't seem do much to lighten my dark thoughts, though. Then I developed terrible abdominal pain. It felt like my insides were being torn apart. Sometimes I even vomited blood."

"That's terrible," I said, shaking my head. "Those pills were probably making you worse."

"But I just kept taking them, hoping they'd eventually fix me. I remember sitting in a classroom one day listening to the teacher tell story after story about man's inhumanity to man. Of course, that only added to my despair. It hurt to hear all the hateful ways people treated each other. Suddenly, tears started streaming down my face. Of course I was embarrassed, so I sprinted out the door and into the men's room. I stared at my reflection in the mirror, hardly recognizing the stranger with a gaunt face and red swollen eyes. Questions bounced round and round in my head."

"What kind of questions?" I asked.

"Why can't I keep it together? What is wrong with me? What is wrong with this world? Why am I so lonely? Who am I? People are all around, but do I have a true friend?"

"Aw, that's so sad, Paul," I whispered.

"Yeah, I was a mess for well over a year. On my twenty-first birthday, Lauren and my mom drove down from L.A. to take me to a popular hangout close to campus. I forced myself to go, trying to act normal and happy. But I felt abnormal and empty the entire time. To me, people in the bar were just puppets playing their parts, trying to cover up their own fears and loneliness. I smiled and nodded when spoken to, but I had no interest in what anyone was saying."

"Did you finally get some help?"

"Yes. Help came in the form of a weird feeling one morning early in my junior year. I woke up to an overwhelming urge to get out of bed. Something was compelling me to hurry, get dressed, and leave the dormitory. It was as if I had no choice, but to trust where my feet were taking me. My senses seemed heightened; I noticed things in vivid detail, as if seeing them for the first time."

"Really? What kind of things did you notice?"

"The beauty of things I'd been missing—nature, the plants, trees, sun shining on the leaves. Then I allowed my feet to lead me up the concrete staircase of a building. It was the counselors' office. When I walked through the inner door, I saw a woman typing at the reception desk. She looked up, and asked if she could be of assistance.

"My eyes welled up with tears. But somehow I managed to blurt out that I needed help. The woman smiled and asked my name. When I told her, she led me to a group of empty chairs, saying someone would be right over. Sure enough, a gray-haired man walked up to me. He looked friendly . . . like he could be anybody's father."

"Who was he?" I asked, caught up in the story.

"He introduced himself as Mr. Ludwig, a counselor for undergrads. I followed him to his office. He sat behind his desk leaning forward to give me his full attention. After we talked in general for awhile, I started opening up to him about the pain I'd been struggling with for so long."

"What did he say?"

"He said he'd like for us to talk on a regular basis. So he set up a schedule for me to come to his office twice a week. He took me under his wing. He was surprisingly caring and supportive, as well as professional during our appointments. And, what a relief it was to have him to talk to."

"What were some of the things you talked about?"

"I told him how important the Golden Rule was to me," Paul answered. "We also spoke about the necessity of accepting others and ourselves for who we are, because it's the only way to live honestly. And we discussed how giving to others is truly the way to receive, which goes hand in hand with love thy neighbor as thyself."

"It sounds like he understood you, Paul."

"He did. I began to value his friendship immensely. He invited me to his beautiful home, treated me to a couple of symphony concerts, and drove me in his new Cadillac. But I was most impressed when he told me he carried absolutely no debt. He paid cash for everything. That was so different than what I had grown up with. Many times our family cars had been repossessed right out of our garage. My father believed that even if you were broke you should look like a king."

"So, how long did your meetings with Mr. Ludwig continue? And, did you feel like you achieved some kind of breakthrough from his counseling?"

"I saw him regularly for over a year and a half—until I graduated," Paul answered. "And I did have a breakthrough. It happened the day he put his hand on my knee, telling me how proud he was of all the hard work I'd done and how far I'd come since our first meeting. He admired how much I cared about others, and hoped I'd always honor that gift, because I had a lot of love to give."

"How did that make you feel?"

"I was stunned," Paul replied. "No one had ever said anything like that to me before. I replayed his words in my head for days, feeling hopeful about the future—something that I hadn't felt in a long time. The darkness lifted as I saw myself in a new way. And that's when I vowed to live my life loving thy neighbor as thyself, and treating others as I'd want to be treated—following the Golden Rule."

"Ah, some basic tenets of Bio-Touch," I said with a smile. "But those were lofty goals for anybody, let alone such a young man. How did you put that vow into action?"

"Well, I forced myself to attend parties despite how uncomfortable all the superficial chatting made me feel. Instead of thinking of myself, I simply shifted my focus to other people's feelings. I asked them about themselves or what they thought of things, paying close attention to what they answered. Sadly, many were unaccustomed to having some-one really listen to them."

"And what insights did you gain from doing that?"

"I realized that most people were in the same boat I was in. They were insecure, lonely, and scared. They were looking for acceptance and love. As I worked to understand their feelings and fears, I had less time to dwell on my own. I opened my heart to people and accepted them for who they were. Then I realized that I could finally accept myself with that same open heart. That's when I flushed my remaining tranquilizers down the toilet; I knew I'd never need them again. I had touched the depths of despair. But in the midst of that despair, I'd found the pure light of love."

"That's a profound lesson to learn so early in your life," I marveled. "Most adults—myself included—are still trying to figure that stuff out. So, what did you do after you accepted yourself for who you were?"

"I became a resident assistant in my dormitory, counseling the students who needed help. Then I joined the United Farm Workers movement. I liked how the union leader, Cesar Chavez, employed non-violent methods in his approach to unionism. He organized protests and boycotts to try to establish safer working conditions and higher wages for farm workers. I took part in some of those protests, and even had the honor of meeting Cesar Chavez during a protest rally. When he delivered his inspirational speeches, he was actually talking about loving and respecting others. But I was disappointed in the attitude of many of the members of the movement who were not getting that loving message. There was so much dissention and arguing, that I eventually quit attending the meetings."

"What else did you do?"

"I landed a summer job running a day camp for elementary aged kids. The camp was next to a lake that provided swimming and other water-related activities for the campers. As usual, I loved working with the kids, teaching them, and helping them solve their problems.

"But when I found out that the lake was going to be drained for construction of a new planned community, I was upset that the quality of the camp would be severely diminished. I had to do something, so I rallied the campers, as well as their parents, to make protest signs. We began picketing in front of the housing development's corporate offices. The protest grabbed the attention of the local news media, and the negative publicity caused the president and CEO of the housing corporation to invite me to a meeting to discuss the situation. I was happy to be invited to what I hoped would be a sensible exchange of ideas."

"And was it?"

"No. The meeting was a joke. The big-wigs wanted to intimidate me. They demanded that I lie to the protesters. They wanted me to say we'd had a good meeting, were on the same page, and the protest was over. Instead, I walked out of the so-called meeting, told the protesters exactly what happened, and warned that their lake was going to disappear. Then, I was promptly fired by the camp director who didn't want any more trouble. And in the end, the construction project continued as planned."

"Naturally," I said.

"But I knew I'd taught the campers something important about making their voices heard against an uncaring corporate system. And my own long-held negative opinion of the way 'the system' works was further confirmed," Paul said, getting to his feet.

I smiled, realizing he'd been answering my questions for over two hours. "Thanks, Paul. We covered a lot of material for our first day."

After he left, I sat at my desk lost in thought for a long time. It boggled my mind that Paul had suffered with severe depression continuing into 1972, the same time I was grieving the death of my boyfriend, Lory. Paul had been fortunate, though. The universe had directed his feet toward a caring counselor who threw him a lifeline when he needed it most.

Unfortunately, I'd received no such lifeline at my school. When I dragged myself into the health center on the campus of the University of Cincinnati to see if someone could help me through my raw grief, I was turned away. A mental health professional listened to my story with a poker face. Then he spent less than two minutes telling me there was nothing he could do for me.

"You just have to go home and grieve. It's a process that takes time. You're young; you'll meet someone new. Time heals all wounds . . . you'll see," he said, as he showed me the door.

Recalling that sad scene stirred my anger. That person offered me nothing but trite sayings. I was a scared, depressed, vulnerable girl. Where was his compassion? He didn't know what kind of support system I had, or if I had anyone to talk to. For all he knew, he could have been my last hope in the world. Maybe he was new to the job; he was a fairly young man. Or maybe I caught him on a bad day. Either way, I could only hope he changed careers after I left his office that day.

Fortunately, I did have a support system of caring people in my life. Two of them were especially heaven sent—as Paul's counselor was—dispatched at the right time to help me through the darkness. One of them was the cantor at Lory's Temple. (A cantor is someone who leads the congregation in the singing of prayers.) He was a close friend to many of his congregants, and he had known Lory well. Understanding I was grief-stricken, he volunteered to counsel me. For months, he took time out of his busy schedule to visit me at my sorority house one or two days a week. We'd sit alone in the living room, where he encouraged me to talk about my feelings. Sometimes he placed an empty chair in the middle of the room. Then he told me to pretend Lory was sitting there. I was supposed to talk to Lory, telling him all the things I never got a chance to say to him. At first, I was self-conscious, and felt silly talking to the empty chair. But once I started the conversation, the words continued in emotion-filled torrents. That exercise proved valuable in erasing some of my pain.

The other person who came into my life when I desperately needed him was a young man named Howard. A mutual friend, Belinda, set us up on a blind date after warning him to keep conversation on the lighter side because my boyfriend had died six months earlier and I was still sensitive. I wasn't sure I was ready to date, again, but I liked Howard's rich, deep voice when we spoke over the phone.

Belinda and her date joined us as we walked to the movie theater close to campus. *Deliverance,* starring Burt Reynolds, was the main attraction. We had no idea what that movie was about, but it would have been a horrible choice for anybody's first date. Throughout the gory and disturbing film, I cringed and squirmed as if I was sitting on worms. Howard seemed embarrassed, too.

Relieved when the house lights came on, we hurried outside. Belinda and her date went to get something to eat, while Howard and I walked to his dormitory to play ping-pong and talk. Later, as he walked me back to my sorority house, he asked if I would accompany him to a *Jethro Tull* concert that was going to be held soon in Columbus, Ohio. I told him I would love to, but since Columbus was almost two hours away by car, I would have to check with my parents.

Happy to see me getting back into the social world, Mom and Dad told me I could go. However, they wanted to meet Howard, first. I arranged for us to drive together to my folk's house—a half-hour trip—the following Sunday for introductions. But that meeting never took place. Instead, on that day, my mother and I sat in the emergency room of a hospital while doctors tried unsuccessfully to save my father's life.

Howard had known me for only two weeks, yet he attended the funeral, arriving alongside my sorority sisters. After I introduced him to my mother, sister, and brother-in-law, he stood beside my father's open casket for a moment, to pay his respects. It was the first and last time he would ever see his future father-in-law.

After the service, the casket was closed and draped with a burial flag befitting Dad's military service. At the cemetery, soldiers folded the flag into a triangular shape and handed it to my mother. A bugler played *Taps* as Dad's coffin was lowered into the ground. Even through my tears, I could see Howard wiping his eyes.

Forty years later, it still amazed me how that nineteen-year-old man, whom I hardly knew, had voluntarily embraced the broken young woman I was. He patiently listened to my words of pain for months on end. His dark, soulful eyes shone with the depth of his compassion. He could have been out enjoying life dating fun, happy girls who weren't laden with emotional baggage. Instead, for reasons I'll never know, he chose to stay by my side.

As I ambled into the kitchen to make dinner, I mulled over how Paul and I were rescued by loving, caring people during the bleakest hours of our lives. And our rescues had happened at the same point in time.

But Paul overcame his sadness and pain. He became a better person for it, instead of blaming or using it as an excuse. He was led in a new direction after basking in the light of his counselor's love and compassion.

Maybe I needed to take a page from his book, and let go of the resentment I'd been carrying around for so many years. Although grateful for my blessed life, I still maintained a small, ugly place, deep inside, where I begrudged the love denied me when Lory and Daddy died.

But what good was that doing? Was it just an excuse to fall back on when I wanted to feel sorry for myself? Either way, from now on, I was going to focus solely on the years of love my husband, children, and so many others had given me—and were still giving me. That love had been trying to shine its healing brilliance into the darkest corner of my soul for a long time.

CHAPTER SEVEN

The Future Beckons

When you live in the present, the past is forgotten
and the future takes care of itself.

—Mandy Hale

The Single Woman: Live, Love, and a Dash of Sass

Paul was back at my house the following Thursday for our next session. Again, I sat with plenty of paper and pens to capture all the juicy nuggets I was sure to hear. Even though my digital recorder was rolling, I never quite trusted it.

"So, it was 1973, and you just graduated from college when we left off last week," I reminded Paul. "Please talk about your life after that."

"Well, I bought my first house east of Balboa Park in San Diego with a modest down payment borrowed from my mother. The house was small, old, and inexpensive. My girlfriend, Lauren, moved in with me, and we adopted Copey, a German Shepherd-mix puppy from the pound.

"I got a job as a teacher's assistant in a nearby elementary school and took classes in meditation, yoga, and various eastern philosophies. It all worked well for over a year, but then Lauren and I broke up, and she moved out."

"Why? What happened?" I asked.

"We were still close friends, but we'd drifted apart romantically. Lauren was ready to date someone new. While I was trying to get over the breakup, Lauren's sister sent me a book she thought would help me."

"Did it help?"

"It sure did. The book was called *Be Here Now* by Ram Dass, and it changed my life, as clichéd as that might sound."

"I've never even heard of it. How did it change your life?" I was intrigued.

"The book was a simplified explanation of Eastern philosophy. The author, Richard Alpert, PhD, was an American professor of psychology at Harvard, who had worked with Timothy Leary. After Alpert was thrown out of Harvard for his experimental work with the drug LSD, he traveled and studied in India, where he successfully expanded his spiritual consciousness."

"But I thought you said the author's name was Ram Dass."

"His Indian guru gave him the new name of Ram Dass. The book became a counter-culture bible on how to live joyously one hundred percent of the time," Paul continued. "It influenced the American hippie movement, teaching spiritual seekers that true love and enlightenment can only be obtained through being aware of our egos. When we can observe our own egos, the power that those egos have over our desires and actions, wanes. The book also stressed that if we're agonizing about the past or worrying about the future, we're not fully living in the present."

"Well, that's the truth, but it's really hard to stay in the present," I said. "So, is that why the book spoke to you?"

"Yes. Right from page one I could feel its message connecting deeply within me. At first I was concerned I wouldn't be able to truly get its meaning. But when I finished reading the second to last page, I pointed my finger toward the ceiling and exclaimed, "Mmmm!""

"Why'd you do that?"

"Because I got it! It was my 'a-ha' moment. And when I turned to the last page, I was shocked. I couldn't believe it. There was a single word on that page, and it was 'Mmmm!'" Paul laughed with delight.

"Wow, you certainly were in sync with that book," I said, "but how did understanding its message affect your life?"

"It helped me see everything differently—including my break-up with Lauren. Instead of allowing myself to be depressed or angry, I developed the attitude that I didn't really lose Lauren. She was still my friend, and I actually gained an additional friend: her new boyfriend. That was the healthiest way to look at it. And the pain of the breakup was gone as soon as I stopped allowing my ego to dictate my thoughts."

"Wait a minute. Let me get this straight," I said with an involuntary smirk. "You were able to believe that your ex-lover's new lover was now your new friend? No way. I think you were secretly glad to be rid of her."

Paul shook his head, chuckling. "No, no. You'd be surprised how easy it is, with some practice, to look at things outside of your own ego."

"Well you're right about that. I'd be very surprised. I think most people could practice all day, every day, and not be able to do that," I said. "So then what happened?"

"I became disillusioned with my assistant-teaching job. The other staff members tried to dissuade me from becoming too involved with the children—especially the 'problem' kids. But the most enjoyable aspect of the job was encouraging and listening to those kids. I especially enjoyed bonding with them in the lunchroom. That's where we traded stories, jokes, and sandwiches.

"Then one day, the principal called me into his office, warning me not to be so friendly with them. He said I could lose my professional edge as well as my job. But I knew that those kids were exactly the ones who needed me the most. It was just another example of 'the system' and how cold and impersonal it could be."

"So, did you take the principal's advice?"

"Of course not," Paul said with a grin. "In fact, I continued spending extra time with those kids, watching them blossom from the attention. And at the end of the school year, I quit the job. There was no way I was going through another year fighting the small-minded people in the school. When I handed in my resignation, the principal actually had the nerve to say he was disappointed to see such a 'caring employee' leave."

"As if a caring employee had a choice. What a jerk," I said. "So, what came next?"

"I took a summer job as assistant director of the teen program at Camp Scotmar—the camp I had attended and worked at when I was younger. Scotmar had relocated to a former dude ranch on six hundred acres in Mancos, Colorado. Copey and I drove out there in my '67 Volkswagen bus, and I immediately fell in love with the beauty of the area.

"The people I worked with at the camp were dedicated to the well-being of kids, which was a refreshing change after the year I'd had at the school. I was happily in my element, so the summer flew by. But in late August when it was time for me to say goodbye to the campers, I realized I didn't want to go home. And, on the drive back to San Diego, I couldn't stop thinking about Colorado. By the time I pulled into my driveway, I realized that nothing was keeping me in San Diego. I decided it was time to put my house on the market."

"Just like that? You were that sure?"

"There was no question in my mind." Paul's tone was emphatic. "I felt like I was being drawn in that direction. And I knew the time was right. Actually, when I first bought that house I had set a goal for myself to never allow a house to own me. I always wanted to be working towards being mortgage-free. And I always wanted to be able to leave someplace when I felt the time was right. So, by early June of 1975, I'd tied up loose ends, completed all my classes, and sold my house. Then I sold or gave away most of my belongings."

"Really? Why?"

"Because, after studying various philosophies, I realized how much I liked the idea of living a simpler life, a life without unnecessary stuff to weigh me down physically or mentally."

"Oh, I see." I was lying; I didn't really see. In fact, it made me uneasy to even think about parting with my possessions. I'd spent years collecting and amassing things without questioning the practice. It just seemed to be the natural order of things as one got older and the budget got looser. If I saw an interesting gadget, or heard a commercial touting its ability to lessen the drudgery of chores, I would often buy it. I was only too happy to join the ranks of the other carefree customers.

"So," Paul continued, interrupting my reverie, "I packed my bus with what little remained of my things. Copey jumped in, and we headed back to Colorado. I worked the same job I had the summer before at Camp Scotmar. It felt great to be following my destiny."

"It's amazing you could feel so sure about your decision and your destiny," I said, happy to shift my thoughts away from possessions.

"Yes. My life's been magical that way," Paul admitted, his eyes lighting up. "I've never had to agonize over tough decisions, wondering what I should do next. The right road has always presented itself."

"Gee, that's hardly fair to the rest of us poking around in the dark," I said with a wry smile. "So, how was the trip toward your destiny in Colorado?"

"It was significant." Paul smiled. "First, I headed to Santa Rosa, which was about five hundred miles north of San Diego. I wanted to visit Lauren's sister, who'd been my friend for a long time. If you remember, she's the one who sent me the Ram Dass book. She and her husband invited me to stay with them for a few days.

"So I was driving along, when I decided to pick up the first hitch-hiker I saw. And a few minutes later, I noticed a young guy standing on the side of the road with his thumb out. As he climbed in, he said he was going to Santa Rosa. I told him that was my destination as well, so we settled in for the drive. He suggested we stay the night with his friends at a campsite in Big Sur. That was about three hundred and fifty miles away, so I agreed."

"I've heard of Big Sur, but I don't know anything about it. What's it like?" I asked.

"It's a beautiful place on the central coast of California, where the Santa Lucia Mountains drop to the Pacific Ocean. Most of the coast is made up of sheer cliffs. Huge rocks line the area where the land meets the sea. Several rivers join the sea there as well. We arrived there before nightfall, joining his friends around their campfire. As we ate and talked, I was suddenly struck with an epiphany."

"What kind of epiphany?"

"It became clear how those people had absolutely nothing of material value, and probably never did. But I, on the other hand, had enjoyed more than my share of possessions throughout my life. I felt guilty for my good fortune."

"But you'd already given away or sold most of your belongings," I pointed out. "So why did you feel guilty? It's not like you were living high on the hog driving a Mercedes, for heaven's sake."

"That's true, but I still had my bus, my clothes, my books, and some miscellaneous stuff. That was a lot compared to what those people had. So, we spent that night in sleeping bags on the ground. I had a tent in the bus, but since no one else had one, I didn't use mine. When I woke up in the morning, my arm was swollen. I found a tick that had attached itself there and sucked on my blood all night. That bug was bloated to the size of a quarter."

"Ew. See, you should have used your tent. So what did you do?"

"I held my breath and twisted it out of my arm," he said. "No big deal."

"No, of course not."

"Later that morning, the hitchhiker asked me if I wanted to do some acid. I had never done illegal drugs, but I immediately said yes. There was no question in my mind. It was the right thing to do."

"We're talking about LSD here, right?" I asked.

"Yes. I took a quarter tab."

"What's a tab? A tablet?"

"No. Acid tabs were sheets of blotting paper cut into squares, or tabs, which were impregnated with LSD," he explained. "You let them melt on your tongue."

"What did it do to you?"

"The next thing I knew, I was lying on my stomach on the ground staring at the ocean. Then I focused on a single blade of grass growing next to me. That piece of grass became my whole world. I was aware that everything and everybody in the universe was contained within it. Connected together. And that's when I had another epiphany."

"What was this one about?"

"I realized that if I could have that much awareness while using a drug, why couldn't I be in that state all the time? Why not always live my life like that, but without drugs? Then I stood up and walked down to a place where the river met the ocean. I stared at the swirling vortex of water. Then I looked up to see clouds spinning above in another vortex. It was incredible. I stripped off my clothes and jumped into the water. It was the best swim of my life."

"I'll bet," I blurted out. "You're lucky you didn't drown in such a state. No wonder you remember that 'trip' to Colorado so well."

Paul smiled. "I never took acid again. That hitchhiker gave me another tab that I actually carried around in my wallet for two years. But I threw it away; I didn't need it. I'd experienced what it felt like to be totally aware while on LSD. After that, I could gauge my level of aware-ness, always aiming to be totally present without drugs."

"So after your drug trip, you continued on your road trip. What happened in Colorado?" I asked.

"Well, for that entire summer I lived in my tent on the grounds of Camp Scotmar. The job was great; I was happy. And Copey was the per-fect roommate. We hiked for miles, becoming familiar with the sur-rounding landscape.

"When fall came, a friend and I pooled our resources to buy a house. Soon Copey and I were living in our new home with Lenny, his wife, Jeri, and their two children. It was great being part of their family. We ate meals together, shared cleaning duties, and played games. I loved that sense of community I felt living with them. Then one day, Copey and I jumped into my bus to drive back to San Diego to pick up Lauren."

"What? When did your ex-girlfriend come back into the picture?" I asked.

"She and I had remained friends, keeping in touch through letters. In her last letter, she wrote that she had broken up with her boyfriend. Suddenly I could admit to myself how much I still loved her and wanted her back in my life. My half-assed plan was to show up at her door, pro-fess my love, and whisk her to Colorado with me. It was risky; I didn't know if she felt the same way toward me."

"Aw, that's romantic, though," I said. "So, what happened?"

"When Lauren answered the door, she looked shocked. She didn't know what to say, but her eyes told me everything I needed to know. Within a few weeks she had tied up loose ends, and we were on the road to Colorado.

"We enjoyed living with Lenny and his family for months. Then, we were ready to get a place of our own. We fell in love with an old frame home in Hesperus, Colorado. Located next to the La Plata River, it was nestled in the mountains, and surrounded by pine trees. The house sat far from the road on two-thirds of an acre. And in keeping with my phi-losophy not to be owned by a house, it was affordable.

"So, after selling my half-interest in the other house to Lenny, I bought the place in Hesperus. But there was a problem with the property next door. Our new neighbors lived in an old, run-down mobile home that was located a mere fifty feet from our shared property line. And their yard resembled a garbage dump."

"Oh great," I said shaking my head.

"After asking around," Paul continued, "I found out that my new neighbor was Guy, the town drunk. Guy had lived there like a hermit for decades, until finally marrying a much-younger woman. She had blessed him with three children, but apparently she and the children were rarely seen."

"Well, they sound like perfect neighbors," I clucked.

"So, we settled in, trying to ignore their mess. Lauren took a job as a bank teller. I did odd jobs, including working with sheet rock on construction sites. One day on a whim, I applied for a job as a substitute mail carrier. I was surprised I landed it, because of my long hair and bushy beard. But soon I was enjoying driving around in my bus, getting to know people along my one hundred and forty mile postal route.

"Early one morning while getting ready for work, Lauren and I discovered that we had no running water in the house. We turned on all the faucets and . . . nothing. While I was outside staring at our well, a man approached. He was skinny with a worn, wrinkly face. His overalls were greasy and his boots were splattered with mud. Even his ball-cap was grimy. He took a swig from his beer can, smiled, and introduced himself as Guy, my neighbor.

"He asked if I was having trouble with the well. When I nodded, he explained that the cistern had probably run dry due to the recent drought. Then he turned and walked back to his property. I watched as he returned with a long length of garden hose. The smile never left his face as he stretched the hose from his outside spigot down into my cistern. He told me to leave the hose in place. Then he turned, and walked home again. It took over eight hours to fill that cistern.

"I couldn't believe how generous that was of him," Paul continued. "That was a lot of water. But I was suspicious of such generosity from someone I just met—someone I'd heard nothing good about. I worried what his angle was, and what he'd want in return."

"Well, I can't blame you for that. So, what did he want?"

"Nothing but friendship. Guy never asked for payment or favors in return. In fact when I asked how I could repay him, he waved me off saying that's what neighbors were for. I misjudged him, but I still remained wary for a while.

"He started showing up in my yard, lending me tools, equipment, or his assistance. I really appreciated him; he helped me lay pipes, put up drywall, and tackle other projects. Sure, he was always drunk. His next can of Old Milwaukee was always within reach. But he worked hard, could fix anything, and was patient when sharing his knowledge with me. As we worked, I realized that Guy never had an unkind thing to say about anybody. He didn't judge people, even though he was harshly judged. Most people didn't want to know him because they had no idea how big his heart was."

"Well, that was a good lesson for not judging people," I said. "So what else was keeping you busy at that time, Paul?"

"I still drove my mail route, and several nights a week I attended philosophical and spiritual classes, studying late into the night. Then one day, Lauren and I found ourselves sitting at the kitchen table, calmly discussing how our relationship had changed. We looked at each other and cried, knowing it was over. We realized we wanted different things out of life. We had different goals. No one was at fault; no one was to blame. And there were no hard feelings, this time, when Lauren moved out and headed back to California."

"Did you remain friends?"

"We did. However, I noticed how disconnected I felt living by myself. It helped that Guy came over a lot bringing beer and a kindness I had never experienced in a friend before. In fact, Guy was so caring and supportive I realized—with a jolt—that he was my closest friend. He was the perfect example of someone who lived 'love thy neighbor as thyself' and 'to give is truly to receive' principles. I didn't know it then, but he was the first of three mentors who would teach and guide me along my spiritual path.

"Meanwhile, I invited a friend to stay with me who needed a place. Then another friend needed somewhere to live, so I invited him to move in, too. Then I heard about someone else, so I invited her to join us. Their energy was so invigorating, it just grew from there. I invited a few more friends, as well as some fellow students, to live with us. It was that idea of community living that appealed to me, especially after all the years I'd enjoyed living at the camp and the positive experience I had living with Lenny and his family."

"When you say community living, do you mean like a party house atmosphere?"

"No. Quite the opposite, really," Paul answered. "The use of alcohol and drugs was strictly prohibited. My home evolved into a center for diverse spiritual practices. We even designated one room of the house to be used specifically for music, meditation, and classes. Soon, curious visitors, students, and truth-seekers showed up, as well as teachers of various spiritual practices."

"How did they know about your house?"

"Through word of mouth. We began offering classes and workshops. Some of the other residents and I taught classes, as did the visiting teachers. The topics ranged from yoga and other disciplines to Dances of Universal Peace."

"Dances of what? What are those?" I asked.

"A man named Samuel Lewis, who was born in San Francisco around 1900, envisioned and created the dances to promote peace and joy and taught them to hippies in the San Francisco area in the 1960s. He passed away in 1971, but his dances still live on. They celebrate God in all forms, traditions, and religions. The dances are actually a spiritual practice—a kind of meditation—where dancers move in a circle from partner to partner. The steps are simple, with positive words, chants, and songs. I taught the dances for years."

"Well, they sound interesting," I murmured, thinking how the dances might be fun to learn. But I knew I wouldn't be able to do them with a straight face. If I danced around chanting, I would crack up, annoying all the serious hippies searching for peace. I changed the subject. "So, how many people were actually living in your house by then?"

"Well, people came and went, but the most we had at any one time was eighteen men and women."

"Whoa. That's a lot of people. How were things managed?"

"We shared the cooking and cleaning duties and ate all our meals together, adhering to a strict vegetarian diet. Most of the vegetables were fresh-picked from our backyard garden. After the evening meal, we'd gather in the music room to sing and dance or share spiritual experiences, meditations, new massage techniques, or anything else we found interesting.

"But soon we realized that we needed more living space in the house, even though we had two or three people living outdoors in a teepee and two or three living in an underground shelter we'd dug out. It had a roof made of logs that we covered with tarpaper and dirt."

"Good heavens. It sounds like a bear's den," I said, shaking my head.

"Oh, no. It was pretty nice. It even had a stove inside for warmth. Meanwhile, everyone pitched in to help construct a second story onto the house. Guy taught us the finer points of dry wall, framing, welding, and basic carpentry. With his help, the new upstairs room became the dormitory."

"How many bathrooms did you have, by the way?" I asked.

"In the house? One."

"What? You had one bathroom for eighteen people? And what do you mean in the house? You had one somewhere else?"

"Yes, we had a little outhouse in the yard."

"An outhouse?" I remembered the few outhouses I was forced to use in my life, when the only other option was a row of bushes. Not only did I have to hold my nose against the stench, but there was the fear of slipping through the hole and falling into the waiting pile of human filth.

Seeing my disgusted look made Paul smile. "It was a very nice outhouse. Seriously. We dug a deep hole in the ground, and built the structure using logs. It had a roof, a locking door, and a real toilet seat. And not only that, it was decorated, too. The walls had colorful artwork and photos of spiritual and religious symbols and teachers."

"Really?" I asked, wondering if it was blasphemous to put sacred photos in an outhouse.

"Oh yes. In fact," he added chuckling, "I actually had an epiphany in that outhouse!"

"Another epiphany? No, Paul, not in the john."

"Yes, what better place?" he said, laughing. "One day while I was inside, my eyes rested on one of the pictures that hung on the wall. It depicted a spiritual teacher who was using his hands to bless a group of young people. Suddenly I realized how much I loved everyone. I loved everybody on the planet as if they were my own family . . . as if they were my own children. And I knew that even if I never had biological children, I'd still be a father to many people in my lifetime."

"Wow, that epiphany was lovely. It's just too bad it didn't come to you in someplace nice, like your garden."

Paul smiled. "So, we found some old windows around town and built a greenhouse out of them. We attached the greenhouse to the southern side of our home, which helped heat the place in winter. One of the crops we grew in the greenhouse was alfalfa. It sprouted in five-gallon buckets.

"We also refurbished an old outbuilding on the property to use as a pottery studio, and we constructed a barn-like structure. We raised chickens and goats, which provided our milk and eggs."

"Well, at least you had plenty of fresh food to eat. Did you charge your residents rent? How was money handled?" I asked.

"Most residents developed a marketable skill. Some taught classes. Some practiced midwifery. Others did beading work, hand-sewed teepees, or made pottery from our studio. I taught classes and made wooden stringed instruments called dulcimers. The dulcimers, beaded jewelry, and pottery were sold to the public who were invited onto the property to browse. At least ten of our fireproof, water-resistant teepees were sold each year for four hundred dollars apiece."

"Man, those must have been some nice teepees," I remarked. "That was a lot of money in those days."

"They were very nice, and worth every penny. So each resident contributed forty percent of their earnings to a common account for household expenses. Those without an income or marketable skill volunteered their time working in the house or garden. And the fifty pounds of alfalfa sprouts that our greenhouse produced each week was sold to restaurants and food outlets."

"Very enterprising. I'm impressed at how well-run your community was, Paul. But what were the problems? Come on. There had to be some."

"Well, we didn't have many problems, but occasionally the stress of so many people living under one roof would erupt in arguments between residents."

"You mean in front of the one and only bathroom?" I asked.

"No. Are you still stuck on the bathroom situation?"

"Yes. Sorry, but I can't get past the image of all those people waiting in line, day and night, to shower or pee."

"It definitely would have been a problem for you," he said with a smile.

"I'll say. I always take a long time in the bathroom. I can't help it; I'm high maintenance, you know. Just think of the arguments that would have erupted if I lived there."

Paul rolled his eyes. "No doubt. But to prevent any such arguments, we began to have weekly meetings, giving everyone a chance to air their feelings before resentments reached the boiling point. At first the residents tolerated the meetings, regarding them as a necessary evil. But eventually, we all looked forward to the honest exchange of feelings within the safety of our loving group."

"Uh . . . just how loving was your group, if I may ask?"

"Do you mean sexually?" Paul asked.

"Sure."

"Well, there were no orgies or free love, if that's what you mean. We certainly were not about sex and drugs."

"Really? Wasn't that unusual for a hippie commune?" I asked.

"We didn't like the word commune. Our community—which we eventually named Starlight Village—was a center for a self-sufficient approach to energy and food, inner-denominational spiritual expression, and conscious living. We were spiritual seekers—not a commune for dope smoking, sex-crazed hippies."

"Oh," I said, feeling a tinge of disappointment.

"But not everyone was convinced of our good intentions. A few of our neighbors were suspicious of what we were up to, and regularly called the sheriff on us. He'd come out to the house, but it was okay because we made friends with him," Paul said with a laugh.

"I love the name Starlight Village. Did you come up with that?"

"Truthfully, I can't remember who came up with that name, but in addition to everything else we were doing, we offered Starlight as a home for foster teenagers. We applied with the La Plata County Department of Social Services and were accepted, so four teens were authorized to live with us at any one time. The kids were unwanted, and in crisis—one misstep away from juvenile detention."

"Were you able to help them?" I asked.

"A few were unable to accept our help and love and had to leave Starlight. But most of them benefitted from our caring and attention. Some really flourished, and that was gratifying," he answered.

"I remember the day I sat outside on a boulder facing the house. It was a warm day, and I could hear several residents talking in the kitchen through the open windows. As I looked at our home, I couldn't help but feel proud of what we accomplished."

"What year was that, Paul?"

"It was 1978. In only two years my house had been transformed into a thriving community of people sustaining themselves in a responsible way. And more importantly, we were incorporating the principles 'love thy neighbor as thyself' and 'to give is truly to receive' in our daily practices. And that's when I had another epiphany."

"Is that four of them now? What was this one?"

"I realized that the house wasn't really mine; it was everyone's house. Though I legally owned it, I was simply the caretaker, the vessel allowing things to flow through and around it."

"Well, you sure had plenty of good things flowing."

"Yes we did, but there was more. We decided to take on the challenge of operating the Animas Valley Free School."

"And what was that?"

"It was a non-profit community school that was floundering. We wanted to keep it afloat because it offered an alternative education program, an arts and crafts guild, a dance and music center, as well as a variety of children's classes. The school admitted everyone. It was supported entirely by registration fees, but even those low fees were waived for needy students."

"Were all the classes held in one building?"

"No, they were held in homes, businesses, and other facilities throughout the Durango area."

"What were some of the courses?"

"Yoga disciplines, horsemanship, leather crafting, Tarot card reading, astrology, basic automotive repair, UFOs, beginning guitar, pottery, beginning watercolor, and the study of death and dying, to name a few. Children's classes included art, nutrition, the mountain wilderness experience, singing, and yoga."

"From auto repair to death and dying . . . certainly something for everyone," I said. "Who were the teachers?"

"Many of us were residents of Starlight, but anyone could lead a class. The teachers lived in and around the Durango area. We sought out advertisers for the course brochures, which we wrote, cut, and pasted-up. Each issue contained information on upcoming classes with some artwork, photography, poetry, and community information sprinkled in. We hand delivered the pages to a publisher, and the printed copies were mailed to the greater Durango community several times a year."

"Wow. That was quite a project for all of you to take on."

"Yeah," Paul said, "sometimes I wonder how we got so much done. And even with all that going on, we decided to try running a restaurant in town, called The Hesperus Café. For three months one summer, we baked bread and made béchamel, hollandaise, and other sauces fresh every morning, creating healthy meals for locals and tourists, alike. We worked from six a.m. until midnight. The property owner was the writer Louis L'Amour. He let us hippies have free rent and keep all the profits that summer. But in return, we fed his young, single nephew three meals a day. What a great deal that was. So, each resident—even our foster teens—took turns working restaurant shifts."

"Okay, enough already. I'm tired just hearing about everything. By the way, I don't read Westerns, but even I've heard of Louis L'Amour."

"So I went to see a chiropractor who wanted my advice on how to include a spiritual center within his practice. As I sat in his waiting room before our meeting, I stared at an elderly gentleman sitting across from me. He looked like Merlin the wizard. His hair was pure white; his eyes were dark beneath thick eyebrows. His lips were barely visible between the silvery mustache and beard that grew to the middle of his chest. Though he looked ancient, he seemed ageless in a way, too.

"He was clearly annoyed. He told a woman, talking on the waiting-room phone, to hang up the receiver because he didn't want any granddaughter of his supporting AT&T. I chuckled and told him that

I didn't like big corporations either. He looked at me, his eyes all black and penetrating. I extended my hand, and introduced myself. As we shook hands, he said that everyone called him Grandfather. He gestured toward the woman on the phone, saying that his granddaughter's name was Lisa.

"After some small talk, I invited them both to come and visit Starlight. I doubted they'd come, but a few days later, a Volkswagen bus, older than mine, screeched to a stop in front of the house. Grandfather and Lisa had arrived. I welcomed them and enjoyed giving them a tour of the grounds. They even stayed to share our evening meal. And later, as I watched them drive away, I had no idea that Grandfather would become my second mentor—and play a pivotal role in my spiritual growth.

"I visited Grandfather as often as I could. I looked forward to spending time with him, knowing I could gain a tremendous amount of knowledge. Soon I was studying privately with him."

"What do you mean by private study with him?" I asked. "Was there a fee? What were the topics?"

"We discussed literature, philosophy, spiritualism, the meaning of life. The way he taught excited me. But there was never a fee. I just went to his hotel room and hung out with him for probably ten hours or so a week. But when summer arrived a few months later, he disappeared. He said he was leaving for awhile because he and Lisa were going to do some traveling. I was very disappointed when I didn't hear from him for over four months.

"Then in late autumn, I drove my bus to the auto repair shop for some minor work. I could see that the mechanic was working on a VW bus that looked familiar. Sure enough, there was Grandfather waving and walking over to me. He looked like he expected me to show up.

"He said, 'I've been waiting for you because I want to ask you a question. Do you think you're awake, young man?'

"I felt frozen in place. I couldn't imagine how he knew I'd be bringing my bus there that day. I hadn't even made an appointment. As his eyes burned into mine, I tried to think of how to answer his hypothetical question, then decided to remain silent.

"He finally said, 'Paul, as long as you think you're awake, you're never going to try to wake up. I'll make you a deal. I'll hang out here in

Durango for a while, instead of doing more traveling, if you'll help me hold out my hat on the street corners to collect people's wasted time. Is it a deal?'

"Before I could answer, he started quoting Shakespeare:

'Buy terms divine in selling hours of dross; within be fed, without be rich no more: so shalt thou feed on death, that feeds on men, and death once dead, there's no more dying then.'

"When he finished, I just stared at him with a big smile on my face. I guess I agreed to his deal."

"Sounds like he was quite a character," I said. "So then what happened?"

"I continued studying with him. Soon he began giving philosophical talks in a meeting room in Durango one night a week. That was one of the ways he meant to collect people's wasted time. The price of admission was any three questions someone wanted answered. He drew a crowd."

"Obviously, money wasn't very important to him," I said. "What were his talks about?"

"Money meant absolutely nothing to him. One of the teachings he always emphasized was from the book, *The Perennial Philosophy*, by Aldous Huxley. Grandfather explained that the golden thread of truth tied together all religions, philosophies, and spiritualities. Even though they contained some different components, they were all drawn from the same well of eternal truths.

"So, I'd been studying with Grandfather for about a year when I realized that in order for me to concentrate fully on my spiritual growth I should settle down and get married. I was twenty-eight and in a relationship with a woman named Karyn, who lived at Starlight. Karyn was an artist, as well as the resident potter of our community.

"When I told Grandfather I was ready to get married, he asked, 'Are you sure you want to do this?' He wanted to be sure I understood what marriage was all about. So in the months prior to our wedding, Grandfather counseled me and Karyn, helping us think deeply about the upcoming responsibilities of marriage. He read lots of quotes to us about relationships.

"We wanted our ceremony to be on the vernal equinox, signifying a new beginning. So on the first day of spring in 1979, in a severe snowstorm, Karyn and I were wed. Grandfather co-officiated along with an ordained minister. And despite the weather, many friends, acquaintances, and even some of my mail route customers attended. Unfortunately, the furnace wasn't working in the wedding hall, so the building was pretty cold. But we dressed warmly, ate pot luck dishes, and everyone had a great time.

"After our candle lighting ceremony, flute players and belly dancers joined in our celebration. A guest asked me if this was a traditional Jewish wedding," Paul said, chuckling. "I told her, no, it was a traditional hippie wedding."

"Big difference." I giggled, imagining shocked guests gaping as belly dancers gyrated around jingling their finger cymbals at a traditional Jewish wedding ceremony. "So, did your parents and brother attend your wedding?"

"My dad didn't attend. He was living and working in Hawaii, and since the wedding was on a Wednesday, it wasn't convenient for him to travel in the middle of the week. But I was very happy that my mother and brother showed up. Luckily, they had a jeep to get through all the snow. They just made it through Wolf Creek Pass, the mountain route, before it was closed due to the worsening road conditions."

"So how was life after the wedding, when things had quieted down?"

"It was good. I felt content. And over the next two years, I threw myself into my studies with Grandfather. But I began to realize how the burden of my responsibilities was taking precious time away from my inner spiritual work. Many nights I was too tired from running the restaurant, driving the mail route, or teaching classes, to do much studying."

"What was Grandfather teaching you at that time?"

"Grandfather's lessons centered around two major components. The first was the importance of living as simply as possible—getting down to the basics—which I had already begun to do. The second was the necessity of erasing one's personal history—ridding oneself of the trappings and indoctrinations of modern society in order to fully focus on self-awareness and spiritual growth. Grandfather believed those things were necessary to free ourselves to pursue deeper things."

As I opened my mouth to ask Paul how one went about erasing personal history, he yawned and stretched. The two hours had flown by, and it was obvious that our session had come to an end. That question would have to wait until next week.

Later as I read over my notes, I was struck, just like I was the week before, by a major similarity between our lives. Paul drove from California to Colorado in June of 1975 to begin a new chapter in his life. He was convinced it was his destiny. Howard and I also drove off in June of 1975 to start a new chapter in our lives. We were going from our apartment in Cincinnati, Ohio, to a new apartment in Phoenix, Arizona, ahead of the moving van. Yes, we were starting a new life, too. But we had no indication that it was our destiny. In fact, we just hoped like hell we were making the right decision.

Howard had accepted a position with an accounting firm in Phoenix after college graduation. We just celebrated our first anniversary and thought it would be exciting to move far away from home. Six months earlier, we fell in love with the state after driving a rental car north to the Grand Canyon and south to Tucson, after our flight to Phoenix for his job interview. We were blown away by magnificent mountains, glorious deserts, and of course, delightful weather.

We were young, so moving eighteen hundred miles away from our support system of family and friends felt more adventurous than scary. Though we had mixed feelings, we didn't let that stop us. The excitement of the move was too intoxicating. But I underestimated how tough it would be to acclimate to a new place in which we knew no one. I soon missed my family and friends more than I could have imagined.

Fortunately, we met people through Howard's new company, befriending six or seven couples, and joining their picnics and parties. It was fun chatting with the other wives while we watched our husbands play softball.

After our daughter, Jill, was born we bought our first house. And just like Paul had gotten into his first house, we borrowed a small amount of money from my mother. The tiny three-bedroom home was a former model, so it was nicely decorated with wallpaper and window coverings. It was a great little house in which to start our family.

But although we loved living in Arizona, Howard and I wanted our little girl to know our folks back home and benefit from their love. The few visits a year from them just wasn't cutting it, so Howard put in for a transfer. The closest office to Ohio they could offer at that time was Rochester, New York. So, we sold our house and moved there after having lived in Phoenix for only three years. We lived in Rochester for two years before another transfer took us back to Ohio.

Paul's cross-country move in June of 1975 took him to where he needed to be to meet the right people. Guy and Grandfather, two of his life teachers, would be fundamental to his spiritual growth and, ultimately, his destiny.

My cross-country move in June of 1975, though certainly an opportunity for self-examination and personal growth, didn't seem to align me with my destiny. But when we moved back east, I knew in my heart that Arizona was where we needed to live in our "golden" years. Twenty years later, Howard and I finally moved back to Arizona—to Tucson this time—where I could appreciate what was waiting for an "older" me to discover. Indeed, it was my destiny, too.

CHAPTER EIGHT

Imparting Their Knowledge

The teacher who walks in the shadow of the temple among his followers gives not of his wisdom but rather of his faith and lovingness. If he is indeed wise, he does not bid you enter the house of his wisdom, but rather leads you to the threshold of your own mind . . .

Kahlil Gibran
The Prophet

"Are you kidding me? That's how you erased your personal history? You divorced your family?" Paul was back at my house, a week later, explaining one of Grandfather's main teachings. Erasing personal history was a concept he briefly mentioned the week before.

"Yes. I guess you could call it that. I took a leap of faith," he answered. "I trusted Grandfather, who believed it was necessary to do so. He taught the importance of freeing ourselves from the restrictive boxes that families, friends, cultures, and societies placed us in. We're all manipulated and indoctrinated—told how we should live our lives, and what we should believe. But once we're free from those boxes, we can discover who we really are, and what we're supposed to do while on this planet. Our world, which we take to be truth, is actually a created reality, programmed into us from birth—even by our well-meaning families."

"Well, that may be true, but that's how we're used to living. Created or not, it's all we know," I said.

"Exactly, which is why we need to observe, listen, and question everything. After studying with Grandfather for two years, I realized

99

that to fully embrace the truth, I needed to immerse myself in it full-time. Of course, that would require making major changes to my life, and to my wife's, as well. But Karyn was onboard and excited by the idea, so I decided to make it happen."

"What kind of changes?"

"First, I freed myself from the burden of my many responsibilities. I gave up my involvement in the Animas Valley Free School, and quit my job with the post office. Then I explained to the residents of Starlight that I was selling the house that I had loved for five years, so the community we created would have to be dissolved. It was hard, but they understood why I had to make those changes . . . how important it was for me."

"How important what was for you?" I insisted.

"My need to drop out of society. Karyn and I, Grandfather and Lisa, and a few friends were about to embrace a simple and self-reliant life—without public utilities—otherwise known as 'off the grid.' We were going to live on the land, dedicating our lives to finding God and glory, and focusing solely on Grandfather's teachings."

"Wow, talk about putting your money where your mouth is," I said. "But what did your parents say about that?"

"Well, my dad and brother, Bruce, lived in Hawaii. I flew out to visit them and tell them goodbye."

"You flew to Hawaii to break ties with them? For how long, forever? And wasn't that rather dramatic?"

"I didn't mean it to be dramatic, just honest," Paul stressed. "They knew how I'd been seeking and studying for a long time. I was already thirty years old. I told them I loved them, but I had finally found my path. I didn't know how long it would be, but I was prepared to live that way for the rest of my life. It wasn't an easy conversation to have. But they did their best to accept that it was what I had to do. However, when I went to see my mother, the conversation was much tougher. It was impossible for her to accept what I was saying."

"Well, of course it was," I said. "She was your mother, for heaven's sake."

"Yeah. She cried; she was hurt. She wanted to know how she was supposed to pretend that I didn't exist anymore. She wanted to know how having her in my life precluded me from pursuing my studies."

"Damn good questions," I blurted out. "I'm a mother. If one of my children came to me to say goodbye, possibly forever, I'd be shocked, then pissed off, and then I'd want to go off and die."

"I know. It wasn't easy. But it was necessary."

"I'm sorry, but I'm just not grasping this, Paul," I said. "Why would the study of life's truths require permanent separation from the people who raised you, and loved you all your life? Sure, your family had problems; whose doesn't? But they were good, loving people, right?"

"Of course they were. And I loved them very much, too. But it didn't matter how loving and good they were, or if they were the worst family on earth. I needed disconnection from anything that defined me or kept me restricted within society's faulty beliefs. That's why it was necessary to escape that world—so I could finally recognize the truth.

"You're frowning, Debra. I know you're struggling to understand this," he said. "But believe me when I say that 'dropping out' like I did was necessary to eventually lead a life of service to others for the rest of my time on this planet."

"Well of course I believe you," I said. "You've volunteered your time with the Bio-Touch organization for over twenty years. But may I ask—because my mind just works like this—what if one of your parents had passed away while you were living on the land? You told them goodbye. They were hurt. How would you have handled the guilt?"

"Well," Paul said with rising eyebrows, "those questions are based on assumptions, so they're impossible to answer. They're rooted in fear. You see, when we're scared bad things will happen, we can't act on anything. We're paralyzed with fright. While I was living on the land, I trusted that everything would unfold just perfectly. And it did. Actually, that's how I've lived my entire adult life. Each moment we're with someone, we need to be truly present with that person. Then we can part from them, whether for a short time or forever, knowing we have truly experienced love with them. If we really love each person we're with, we can leave their presence knowing that the relationship is complete. Then we're ready for anything that may happen. We can have faith that the future is taken care of. As Shakespeare said in Hamlet, 'There is providence in the fall of a sparrow.'"

"But what does that mean? I never could follow Shakespeare," I admitted.

"It means God is taking care of everything. Even the death of a tiny sparrow is noted, because it falls within His master design. So, my parents didn't die while I was living on the land. The reality was, I was being prepared to someday be by their sides when they did die, which I was. I even said to my mother in her last days, 'You have one final lesson to teach me Mom . . . how to die.'"

"Whoa, that's heavy," I said. "But I'm happy to hear you had a relationship with your parents later in life. So what happened after you said goodbye to everyone?"

"Starlight sold quickly. I used the money from the sale to create a land holding, otherwise known as a trust. I liked that word better because I liked the idea of trusting people. And as a way of fostering that trust, I gave authorization to Grandfather, Lisa, and three friends who were going to live on the land with us, so they could invest in the trust as well. Then the trust bought thirty-six acres of land outside Durango, Colorado."

"So, did those other people have to terminate relations with their families, too?" I asked.

"Yes, we all had to say goodbye to our families, close friends, and anything or anyone else that could distract us from our purpose."

"But why was it okay to live with those other people? Didn't you have personal history with them? Didn't you create more all the time?"

"Yes, in every moment we create more history, Debra. But it was most important to rid ourselves of the older history that was created by family, friends, and society. You see, those old habits and patterns were the ones that really kept us stuck in those boxes."

"I don't know," I sighed. "I still can't imagine voluntarily saying goodbye to people I loved."

"It was hard, but it was important for us to do at that time."

"Okay, so tell me about the property you bought."

"The parcel of land was located off the highway down a rutted, dirt road. The road led into a valley adjacent to the La Plata River. At the property line, an even rougher private lane stretched half a mile. It ended about a thousand feet from a stone house that was built in the

1890s. At one end of the property was a sloping hill, covered in pinyon pine trees. Sage trees, cottonwood trees, and scrub oak also grew in abundance at that elevation—six thousand feet. Surrounding the property were farmed fields, cleared and planted with beans and wheat. There were orchards close by, as well."

"It sounds lovely."

"It was absolutely beautiful. There was an old-time well that was hand-dug when the house was built. The builders had quarried stone not only for the house, but also to line the well. That well, four feet in diameter and forty feet deep, produced the only sweet water in the valley. The other water in the area had a sulfur smell and taste to it. But our well had been left uncovered, accumulating debris and dead animals for who knows how long? It needed a good cleaning, so Guy and another friend helped me scrub it. It wasn't fun. I tied a rope to my waist so I wouldn't fall in, and used a coffee can to scrape out the crap before dumping it into a bucket. Guy stood there gripping the other end of the rope."

I giggled. "That would have been fun to watch."

"Yeah, I was covered in black muck. After the well was clean, we made a wooden cover for it, stuck a long pipe through it, and placed a red cast-iron hand pump on top. Then we constructed a bridge from nailed-together logs to cover a wash on the private lane. That was necessary because sometimes the river rose so high that the water was too deep to drive through. And after that, we constructed a gate across the opening to the private lane to discourage outside vehicles from driving onto the property."

"Sounds like there was plenty of hard work to do around there."

"Oh, we were just getting started," Paul said. "The next order of business was to make the necessary repairs to the stone house. We fixed up the roof and the floors so Karyn, Copey, and I could move in. The main room had great windows, which brought in a lot of light. And the kitchen area included a sink and a wood-burning stove. A ladder led to the upper loft."

"Uh, is that where the bathroom was?" I asked with a smile.

Paul smiled back. "Prepare yourself. There was no bathroom in the house."

"What? Wait a minute. What year was this?"

"It was 1981."

"And no one had bothered to add a bathroom onto the house in almost a hundred years?"

Paul shrugged. "It was rustic. The land had never even been developed for gas or electricity. There were no water lines, phone service, garbage pickup, or mail service."

"Rustic? You mean primitive."

"That was the point!" Paul exclaimed.

"Oh, yeah. So you moved onto the land. You, Karyn, Grandfather, Lisa, and who were the other three people?"

"My cousin, Sarah, and our friends Cheryl and Kalima. Sarah set up a yurt to live in."

"What's a yurt?" I asked. "I've seen that word in crossword puzzles."

"It's a round, tent-like structure with a canvas top," Paul explained. "Cheryl shared the yurt with her. We'd known Cheryl for years. She used to visit Starlight and also attended Grandfather's talks in town. Our other friend, Kalima, moved into her own homemade teepee. We'd known Kalima at Starlight for years, too. Grandfather and Lisa set up a campsite next to their bus. Then we all settled into our home sites, which were located about a hundred yards apart."

"So put me out of my misery, already. Where did you go to the bathroom?" I implored.

"We built a community outhouse."

"Oh, great. Another outhouse."

"Yes, but this one was a composting outhouse that we constructed out of bricks and cement. There were two private seating areas positioned above two fifty-five gallon oil drums. When the drums filled up, which took a long time, by the way, they were rolled out for cleaning and composting. Used toilet paper was burned, along with other paper garbage."

"Ugh. That thing must have stunk to high heaven. I'm speechless."

"You should be. It was ingenious," Paul said.

"Yeah, well which lucky soul got latrine duty?"

"We took turns, of course."

"Share and share alike," I said with a grin. "So, where did you bathe?"

"You're really obsessed with bathrooms and bathing, aren't you? I think you're too clean, if you want to know the truth. Haven't you read how bathing everyday destroys your skin's protective oils?"

"I'll take my chances," I said. "Besides, that's why they invented body lotion. So you bathed—where?"

"We bathed in the river. We even used biodegradable soap and shampoo so we wouldn't pollute the water. But in colder weather . . ."

"Hold on a minute. You bathed in the river? How do you take a bath in a river? I'm serious, now. I really don't know. Do you soap up and then jump in? Or do you jump in and soap up under water?"

A look of mock surprise came over Paul's face. "You mean you've never been camping?"

"As a matter of fact I went camping with Howard two months before our wedding. I even have pictures to prove it. It was a miserable, hot weekend, but it never occurred to me to bathe in the lake, for heaven's sake."

"Well, you should have. It would have cooled you off. So, did you enjoy yourself at all?" he asked.

"No. Actually, it's a miracle we were still engaged by the time the weekend was over."

"I can only imagine." Paul threw his head back and laughed. "I can't wait to hear that story."

"Well, maybe I'll tell you about it someday. But for now let's keep the focus on you, okay?"

In truth, I was too embarrassed to tell him about that awful weekend in April of 1974, when Howard drove me and a couple of our friends two-hundred miles to Cumberland Falls State Park in Kentucky. It was Howard's idea to go camping, and because I'd never done it, I thought it might be fun. He said I didn't need to lift a finger, that he would supply all the equipment for the two of us.

The scenery was pretty, lush, and green. But the humidity was ninety-nine percent, and the skies were threatening rain. As we set up our camp site, it was obvious that Bob and Sheryl's tent was roomier and of better quality than Howard's old, rundown pup-tent.

We grilled hotdogs and hamburgers for dinner, but the weather killed my appetite. My clammy skin, sweaty clothes, and frizzy hair annoyed me. When Howard and I held hands, the moistness between our fingers made slurping noises.

I didn't think I could endure air any steamier or more stagnant than what we were already breathing, but then Howard and I squeezed into the tent. That stifling sauna must have been designed to accommodate a pair of toddlers. There was no ventilation, and it smelled like moldy cheese. The beds—cheap air mattresses that offered little protection from the hard ground—made whooshing sounds as we tried to get comfortable.

After yawning, Howard said he hoped I hadn't touched the inside of the tent anywhere, because that could be a problem if it rained. When I asked him what he was talking about, he explained that the canvas absorbs skin oils and would no longer be waterproof where it was touched.

Trying to remember if I placed my fingers on the tent, I heard Howard's breathing become slow and regular. He was already asleep. How could he doze off inside that tiny oven? I scratched at the heat rash sprouting on my abdomen—my typical summertime affliction—while listening to nature's nocturnal noises. Who could sleep through those buzzings, hoots, and creaks? And hearing Sheryl and Bob laugh from inside their spacious tent didn't help, either.

I may have drifted off for a while. But then I heard it—the soft patter of raindrops against the canvas. Uh oh. Instantly wide awake, I listened to the rain drumming on the tent. Something cold and wet hit my forehead. I gasped. Damn it, I must have touched the tent! More drips hit me. I'd heard of the Chinese Water Torture, eventually driving victims insane as they anticipated being hit in the forehead by yet another drop of cold water. Now I was living it.

Howard slept peacefully, oblivious to the dozen places rain now trickled inside the tent. Of course, none of the leaks were situated over his face. Unable to stand it a minute longer, I woke him up complaining. But he just turned over, drowsily mumbling that I needed to forget about it and go to sleep. How helpful.

I spent the remainder of that night dodging drops beneath a scratchy, moth-eaten blanket. At some point I needed to use the restroom, the urgency made worse by the sound of cascading water. But there was no way I was going to crawl out those tent flaps, and traipse through that muddy monsoon. Somehow I managed to endure the rest of the night without strangling my fiancé in his sleep.

When I awoke, the rain had stopped. I was alone. I emerged from the tent blinking blood-shot eyes and rubbing my aching back. I wore the damp, bedraggled top and shorts I'd slept in. My face was streaked with yesterday's makeup, while ringlets of hair, defying gravity, bobbed around my head in a fuzzy halo.

I frowned when I spotted Howard, Bob, and Sheryl cutting up fruit for breakfast. As they chatted quietly, their glowing good looks gave evidence to how well they'd slept. They greeted me, but I couldn't stop to chat. I needed to get to the bathroom before my bladder exploded.

Needless to say, we didn't stay another night. We packed up the campsite, including our soggy tent and blankets, drove back to Cincinnati, and dropped Bob and Sheryl off at their place. By the time Howard pulled into my driveway at home, it was late afternoon. I could see my mom waving from the window after hearing the car's engine.

Howard waved back at her. Then he hugged me, and suggested I go into the house, take a shower, and grab a nap. I must have looked as disgusting as I felt. He said he'd call me later. Putting the gearshift into reverse, he waited for me to jump out. He was obviously anxious to leave, but I didn't want him to go, yet. I asked him to come inside and stay a while, but he shook his head saying he wanted to get back to his place to clean up and run a few errands.

Something about his polite, sensible refusal threw me into a rage. I morphed into a five-year-old in the midst of a temper tantrum. Roiling with frustration, I kicked my foot harder than I intended, then watched in horror as my shoe made contact with the dashboard of Howard's beloved '67 Plymouth Belvedere. Reacting to the loud crunch, I yanked my foot back from the now dented dashboard. It sagged pitifully on one side, torn from the seam that ran next to the glove compartment.

Seeing Howard's stunned expression made me feel even worse. I tried to find the words to apologize, but he didn't want to hear them. He just kept shaking his head, staring at the damage. To his immense credit, he managed to stay calm. I tried to hug him, but he pulled away from me. Who could blame him? Other men, I'm sure, would have called off the engagement at that point, glad to be rid of the psycho who kicked in their dashboard. But thank heavens Howard forgave me. We remained engaged and got married two months later, as planned. However, even though I never lost my temper to the point of inflicting damage on anything, again, Howard never suggested we go on another camping trip!

My thoughts returned to the present in time to hear Paul say, "So, the river was about ten feet across, but only knee-high where it flowed by our homes. In order to bathe, we just sat down in the water, soaped up, splash rinsed, and toweled off. Just that simple."

"Were you naked?" I asked.

"Yes, people are usually naked when taking a bath. Oh don't look so shocked. There was no one else around but us. So who cared?"

"Okay, so modesty wasn't important to hippies. But weren't you just as dirty after sitting in that shallow river water?"

"No. Believe me, we got clean enough," Paul said. "But if we wanted to bathe in deeper water, we walked downstream to where beavers had built dams. The dams created pools to swim in that were four or five feet deep."

"Well Calgon, take me away!" I exclaimed. "Who wouldn't want to bathe in the nude with large, buck-toothed rodents? I just read in the paper about a rabid beaver that bit three people in a park in Philadelphia. That wouldn't have been a fun thing to happen with all your parts hanging out under water."

Paul laughed, shaking his head. He took a long sip of water from his green bottle. "We never bothered the beavers, and they never bothered us. Now, when winter came, we actually took baths inside our homes. We heated five gallons of water on our stoves, and poured the hot water into our personal aluminum stock tanks."

"Stock tanks like the ones for farm animals to drink out of?" I asked.

"Yes, but they weren't big ones. They only measured four feet in diameter and stood about a foot high. You could get surprisingly clean in them, though."

"A foot high with only five gallons of water? I doubt it," I snorted. "And how did the women shave their legs in those tanks?"

"They didn't shave. They didn't use makeup or beauty products, either. Those women were completely natural," Paul said, a proud tone to his voice.

My nose wrinkled, assaulted by an imaginary whiff of body odor. "Personally, I've never been all that impressed with natural. Sasquatches are natural, too, you know. A few cosmetics and some deodorant can make a world of difference for everybody," I sniffed. "So how did the others, who didn't live in your house, heat their bath water?"

"They each had a sheepherder, a small wood stove with a pipe that vented through the roof."

"Through the roof of a yurt, a bus, and a teepee?"

"Oh yes," Paul answered. "The yurt and teepee were designed for that, and Grandfather rigged the stove pipe through the window of his bus."

"And where did you do laundry—back at the river?"

"No. A few dirty items at a time were placed in a plastic, five-gallon bucket. The bucket's lid had a plunger-type stick. After the water and bio-degradable detergent was added, the plunger was moved up and down, agitating the clothes until they were clean. Then they were hung outdoors on clotheslines to dry."

"That's a lot of work for a few clothes. What if it was cold?"

"In winter, those hanging clothes froze stiff as boards. Freeze-dried," Paul said with a laugh.

"What if it was raining or snowing or hailing?" I persisted.

"It took a lot longer for them to dry."

"Sounds like you were living in one of the nine circles of hell."

"We loved it."

"Of course you did," I said shaking my head. "So, what did you eat?"

"We planted a large garden with carrots, beets, bell peppers, tomatoes, squash, lettuce, and Swiss chard. Whatever we couldn't eat right away was stored in our newly built root cellar for the winter. When the nearby orchard's trees were ripe with fruit, we cleaned up the grounds around the groves. In return, the owners gave us permission to pick all the fruit we wanted. Any extra fruit was covered with straw and buried in the ground, which kept it in great condition for months. We even made a hydrator out of window screens to dry the fruit. Extra apples were made into applesauce."

"Please don't tell me you used compost from your outhouse to fertilize the crops in your garden."

"Okay, I won't," Paul said, his eyes twinkling.

"Ugh, weren't you worried about getting diseases found in human waste?"

"We never worried about it, and we never got sick."

"Okay." I sighed, "So, what'd you do when you got tired of eating fruits and veggies?"

"We developed a barter system with our neighbors. They gave us fresh milk and eggs, bags of wheat, and pinto beans in exchange for toiling on their farms. We did backbreaking work, cleaning out irrigation ditches, clearing the land of rocks, and throwing sixty-pound bales of hay onto wagons. Even Grandfather 'bucked' those hay bales and helped us pick up rocks.

"And we always looked forward to autumn, when the pinyon pine trees around our property produced cones," Paul added. "We propped a ladder against a tree, climbed up, and shook the limbs. The nuts would fall out of the cones, collecting in a tarp. We roasted the nuts in our stoves, and then cracked them open to release the meat. Delicious."

"Now, that does sound good," I admitted.

"After a while, Cheryl was ready to move out of the yurt she shared with Sarah and build her own log cabin by hand. She said she always wanted to live like the pioneers did. So she bought logs and stripped them of bark using a two handled draw knife and lots of elbow grease. The rest of us helped her build the roof and install the wood plank floors. And in four months time she moved into her new two story, twelve by twelve foot house."

"Wow. It's amazing that she built her own house—and without power tools. She must have been one tough cookie," I said. "As a kid I watched the terrible lives of pioneers on television shows like *Wyatt Earp* and *Gunsmoke.* Even then I was grateful to be born in the time of hair dryers and air conditioning. So, did Cheryl's house have a kitchen?"

"Well, it was more like a cooking area than a kitchen. She could cook and bake bread in the wood-burning stove she bought. The stove heated the house, too. Near the stove was a sink large enough to wash a few dishes in, with water that she hauled from the well. The water would just drain out the bottom of the sink, into a bucket. At night Cheryl climbed a ladder to her second floor loft where she unrolled her sleeping bag and slept on the floor."

"But what if she had to go to the bathroom in the middle of a freezing, snowy night?"

"We all used buckets as chamber pots when necessary."

"Wow. All the comforts of a medieval prison," I said. "But wasn't Cheryl freezing upstairs with the stove downstairs? And what did she use for light if she wanted to read in her sleeping bag until midnight?"

"The stoves provided heat throughout our homes for hours. We kept warm. We wore layers, and our sleeping bags were down-filled. We used kerosene lamps for light, but no one read until late," Paul explained. "In fact, most nights we all turned in as soon as it got dark."

"Why? That could have been six or seven o'clock at night."

"Because we were exhausted. Our days began before dawn. We used that time for private meditation, reading, and studying. Then there were full days of maintenance around the property. The garden needed tending, the firewood needed to be chopped, and water needed hauling. That was on top of the work we needed to do on the farm or in the groves.

"But Sunday evenings were reserved for Dances of Universal Peace," Paul continued. "We all gathered outside the stone house, or inside it, if the weather was foul. I strummed a guitar or played the dulcimer. Cheryl accompanied me on flute or kept the beat on a drum. Karyn, Sarah, Kalima, and Lisa held hands and moved together singing with the music. Even Grandfather joined in."

"It sounds like you had some fun when you weren't chopping wood or meditating."

"We did, but we were a community of people seeking spiritual enlightenment and a simpler way of living. We embraced a Zen Buddhist moral code of non-violence to live peacefully among nature. We respected the eagles, raccoons, skunks, deer, elk, foxes, and other wildlife around us. We refused to kill any living things. So if we saw bugs or rodents in our homes, we either ignored them or took them outside as gently as possible. Even the occasional rattlesnakes we found indoors were humanely trapped and released away from our home sites."

"Rattlesnakes got in your homes? No, thank you! And you ignored the rodents? Weren't you afraid you'd get bitten while you slept on the floor?"

"No, we didn't worry about the rodents. But some of our guests didn't appreciate them very much," Paul said with a smile. "I was chopping firewood one day, when I spotted a late-model luxury car easing down the lane. It stopped in front of the driveway gate, and my father climbed out. We hadn't been in contact for over a year, so I welcomed him with a hug. He said he asked around town for directions to my place. I showed him around the property, and introduced him to Karyn, and everyone else.

"Dad shared our evening meal, and then Karyn and I invited him to stay the night in our home. There were several teepees set up around the property for guests, but we thought he'd be more comfortable in our house. We made a bed of blankets for him on the main floor.

"When I got up early the next morning, and climbed down the ladder from the loft, I saw that dad was already dressed. He looked tired; even in the pre-dawn darkness I could see his eyes were puffy. Over coffee, he said that since I had no mail or phone service, he came personally to see if I was okay. Then he said he was impressed with what he'd seen, and this way of life seemed to suit me. I invited him to stay for a while.

'I'd like that,' he said. 'I'll stay a few days. But I have to check into a motel. I couldn't get a wink of sleep with mice running over me on that floor all night!'"

"Are you kidding me? Come on, that's seriously insane, Paul." I tried to imagine how I would have survived being a member of that loony community. I pictured myself skinny and frostbitten, with greasy hair and braided armpits, whacking rodents out of my teepee with a dulcimer.

"That's just the way it was," he said with a laugh.

"But why weren't you angry with your father for showing up like that?" I asked. "Why didn't you send him away? After all, you were erasing personal history, and he ignored your request for a permanent separation."

"Yes, erasing personal history was the goal, because every moment we're continually creating history, and it takes us away from God. Even now, I create personal history every day, and every night I try to erase it. It's like the spiritual teacher Jiddu Krishnamurti said, 'To live completely, wholly, every day as if it were a new loveliness, there must be dying to everything of yesterday, otherwise you live mechanically, and a mechanical mind can never know what love is or what freedom is.'

"I wasn't angry at my father. He was welcome on the land. You see, since we had no mailbox or telephone, it was easy to live in the present moment there. So anyone who visited us was also living in the present and not influenced by old patterns of personal history. That's why family and friends were welcome. When I said good-bye to my family, I didn't say they couldn't come see me. I explained it was just the philosophical idea of being inaccessible, but within reach. The metaphor I used was being like a rabbit—you never know which bush it's going to pop out from. I was saying goodbye to their world."

"Okay. I think I get it . . . except for the rabbit part," I said shaking my head.

"My father actually visited a few more times, but my mother wouldn't come to the land at all. She was too hurt. Instead, she went into Durango to visit with Karyn, who worked in a pottery studio in town. I remember Grandfather asking me if I was hurt by my mother's actions. I wasn't; I was sorry for her pain, but I couldn't deviate from my commitment to stay put on the land."

"Well, I can't blame your mother for not visiting you on the land," I said. "She was smart to visit your wife to find out about you, though. In that way, she honored your request for separation, but still showed you she was pissed off. I love that. A little while ago you mentioned having teepees set up around the property for guests. Who were your guests?"

"Besides occasional family members, our guests were curious travelers who hiked or drove by the property, stopping to look at our unusual dwellings. They were surprised by our hospitality, because we'd invite them to share our meals and stay in one of the teepees. If they wanted or needed to stay longer than one night, we allowed them to. But they had to agree to help with daily chores in order to earn their keep. Some people stayed with us for months.

"And every other week or so, Guy visited. I was always glad to see him. We'd sit together, talking and sharing his six-packs of beer. Sometimes Grandfather sat with us. Guy didn't always understand Grandfather's abstract commentary, but when the older man spoke, Guy nodded his head respectfully, raising his beer can as if punctuating Grandfather's words. It always made me smile when I saw Grandfather and Guy together. In manner and appearance, they were as different as night and day. But I knew their hearts had the same capacity for loving others, and I deeply appreciated having those teachers in my life."

"Did each resident of the community study with Grandfather?"

"Yes. His role was teacher and spiritual leader for everyone in the community. Our regular study sessions with him were on Sundays. On those days, we'd eat our morning meal together before attending class. Our homework consisted of reading and memorizing passages from Stewart Edward White, Walt Whitman, Shakespeare, the Old Testament, the New Testament, George Gurdjieff, Peter Ouspensky, Socrates, and Plato, to name a few."

"Oh, just some light reading, huh?" I joked.

"Well, Grandfather was well-read, and it was his passion to share his knowledge with people who truly wanted to learn. He always urged us to focus on living deliberately in the moment."

"How were you supposed to accomplish that?"

"We became consciously aware of our daily living. We concentrated on what we were actually seeing, smelling, hearing, touching, or tasting. Regardless of whether we were sweating through chores, eating, watching a spectacular sunset, or taking walks, we strove to do everything mindfully and savor each experience."

"What do you mean by doing things mindfully?"

"It's doing them while being aware of the present moment, but without judging the inner experience. It's observing our thoughts and feelings from a healthy distance; it's self-observation. It's being self-aware, which you know is so important in Bio-Touch. And it's being aware of our attitudes, thoughts, behaviors, and reactions and their effect on our relationships with others.

"Also, Grandfather encouraged us to embrace Henry David Thoreau's book, *Walden Pond*," Paul continued. "That book stressed the importance of living simply—not allowing life's excesses to impede our inner progress towards spiritual enlightenment."

"So were you all learning the same things at the same pace?"

"Well, I wanted to learn even more quickly, so I visited Grandfather in the middle of the night. At three o'clock in the morning, I woke up and walked over to see him. Copey followed behind. Grandfather greeted me with a steaming mug of Nescafe instant coffee, and the two of us discussed principles and doctrines for hours. We huddled inside the old bus, keeping quiet so we wouldn't wake Lisa, who slept right outside."

"What do you mean she slept outside?" I asked.

"There wasn't any room to stretch out and sleep inside the bus, so she slept on foam pads next to the bus, bundled in blankets, and beneath a protective tarp. But inside the bus, the kettle stayed hot on Grandfather's stove, supplying us with endless refills of coffee."

"When did Grandfather sleep?"

"Oh, he rarely slept. He didn't believe humans required any more than eleven and a half minutes of sleep per night."

"Eleven and a half minutes?" I asked. "That's a ridiculous number. Who could function on that amount of sleep? Maybe that's all he needed because he drank so much coffee."

"Nah," Paul shook his head. "Grandfather said we were all brainwashed into thinking we needed seven or eight hours of sleep. I don't know how much sleep he got, but he was always wide-awake and eager to answer my many nocturnal questions.

"Grandfather was an author, too. He wrote several five-act plays that highlighted principles such as the Golden Rule and 'loving thy neighbor as thyself.' I felt that his plays should be shared with the public, so I built a portable stage for a puppet theater. Then Cheryl, Lisa, Sarah, and Kalima constructed puppets, painstakingly sewing costumes for each of them. They even sculpted the heads out of clay. Cheryl and I became the official puppeteers.

"The local shopping mall granted permission for us to conduct the puppet shows every Saturday," Paul continued. "We assembled the stage in an open area right in front of a department store. Our shows became pretty popular, too. Children of all ages loved the high-energy performances. But Grandfather's messages, woven into the theatrics, were aimed specifically at the adults in the audience."

"Sounds like fun, but you didn't mention your wife. You said before that Karyn worked in town. Didn't she take part in the puppet shows?"

"No she didn't. Because she drove into town daily, she wasn't around as much as the rest of us. Being an artist and potter, she rented space in a studio there, where she created and sold her ceramic pieces."

"Oh. So she lived in the real world and on the land at the same time. How did that work for her?" I asked.

"It worked alright for about two years. Then she told me that living on the land was starting to feel like living on the moon. It became too hard for her; she missed her family and friends too much. She enjoyed the experience, but she wasn't willing to do it any longer. So she moved her things back to town, and we eventually divorced."

"Oh, I'm sorry. That must have been tough," I said. But I was secretly marveling at how long she hung in there. I pictured her lapping up the delights of civilization, ravenously devouring a cheeseburger, fries, and a hot fudge sundae surrounded by family and friends. Then she'd luxuriate in a full tub of hot, sudsy water, occasionally reaching with her big toe to press the toilet handle down, flushing it again and again, just for fun.

"Yes, it was tough when she left," Paul said. "But the rest of us continued to thrive on the land for two more years, enjoying inner peace and perfect health. It was great to share space and resources with fellow students who relished philosophical studies and the simpler way of living as much as I did. 'Loving thy neighbor as thyself' was something I got to experience every day of those four years. I was able to provide for my own basic needs, yet still spend a significant amount of time on my studies, which was why I was there in the first place.

"All in all, I felt truly blessed; I was living the fantasy that many others could only dream about," Paul said. "But without Grandfather's guidance, I wouldn't have known how to do it correctly. I would have moved onto the land, but I would have brought old personal history, jaded attitudes, and emotional baggage with me. That would have led to a disappointing experience. Instead, Grandfather steered me through an awe-inspiring journey of self-awareness and spiritual discovery."

"Wow. It sure was the perfect experience for you."

Paul grinned. "Yes it was. My fantasy and your nightmare."

A few hours later, I sat down to decipher and type up my notes. Once again, I was surprised to discover how Paul's life and mine had been in sync. On the surface that didn't seem possible, because while Paul enjoyed his Spartan existence on the land between 1981 and 1985, Howard, Jill, and I lived in a comfortable home in a lovely suburb of Cleveland, Ohio. I enjoyed the many duties of a wife and mother, volunteered at Jill's school, and socialized with friends, neighbors, and family. I became pregnant with our son, David, and eagerly anticipated the delights of caring for a newborn, again. I couldn't have been happier. Who knew I was stuck inside a box that—according to Paul—society had placed me in? I was busy, content, and fulfilled.

However, there were those dark moments when I was still haunted by Lory and Dad's deaths from a decade earlier. It hurt to think of the wonderful things in life they missed. Lory never got a chance to graduate from college, have a career, or be a husband and father. My dad never had a chance to give me away at my wedding, or experience the joys of being a grandfather. Their bodies were in caskets underground, but I ached to know where their souls went.

And that's what led me on a path that was similar to Paul's in 1981. I embarked on my own spiritual journey, reading and studying everything on death and dying that I could get my hands on. Back then, there weren't many books on the subject. But I found a few written by authors Elisabeth Kübler-Ross, M.D., Ruth S. Montgomery, and Edgar Cayce. I tried to understand their messages, but I knew I needed more personal instruction. So I signed up for a twelve-week adult education course at the local high school. It promised to introduce me to the unseen spirit world for three hours every Wednesday night. I had no idea what to expect.

On the first night of class I stared, mesmerized, at our teacher. Janet was striking. She was tall and slender, moving with a discernible lightness. Her short dark hair was diffused with silvery wisps that caught the light, and shimmered around her head. However, her eyes were the most extraordinary thing about her. They were huge grey orbs, gleaming like pinballs. Whenever they focused on me, they probed the depths of my soul.

Janet told us things I'd never heard anyone speak of before, such as her ability since childhood to see spirits of departed souls. As a preschooler, she was comforted by invisible friends who were always around her. Those ethereal entities spoke to her, taught her, and guided her as she grew up. She didn't think anything of it; she figured everyone had those kinds of friends. But as she got older, she realized that her parents couldn't see them. Neither could anyone else. Her family laughed and teased her when she tried to talk about her guides.

As Janet told her stories, she spoke in a calm, straightforward way, without resorting to drama. I became fascinated by her and everything she said, while at the same time praying she wasn't nuts. Over the weeks, she guided us through meditation techniques designed to allow us to meet our own spirit guides. After each session, most of the other students felt they connected with theirs, excited to share their experiences with the class. I was envious of them as they described meeting fascinating people. All I saw during my meditations was a pure-white wolf with golden eyes. It looked at me for a few moments and then disappeared. There was never enough time to feel a connection to it, so I didn't bother telling Janet or the class about it.

Not long afterward, though, I dreamed that a huge black panther was stalking me as I slept in my bed. It leaped onto the mattress, saliva dripping from its exposed fangs. It was about to attack my neck, when it suddenly flattened its ears and slunk away. I turned to see the white wolf lying at the foot of my bed, his golden eyes looking into mine. Heart pounding, I woke up knowing he saved me from something terrible.

The twelve weeks of class flew by, leaving me hungry for more of Janet's instruction and insight. So I signed up for the next class, as did most of the other students. That second course included the topics of astral projection and past life regression.

On the first night of that class, Janet asked us to raise our hands if we'd ever experienced flying—using only our own bodies. My hand shot up as I remembered how I used to awaken in the middle of the night when I was four or five. My room was on the second floor, and I would walk to the top of the carpeted staircase, then fly down to the bottom, landing gently on my feet. It was thrilling. So I would climb back up those ten steps, and fly down again. But during the day while wide-awake, I stood at the top of that same staircase, felt the heavy pull of gravity, and was too scared to attempt flight. I hadn't spoken to anyone about that experience since I tried telling my mother when I was a child. Mom told me I was just dreaming, but even then, I knew it was something more.

Several other students had their hands in the air, too. Janet smiled and nodded, saying that many people have experienced the delights of flying, especially as children. She said it was called astral projection—when our souls slipped out of our bodies to travel around the house, around the world, or to other dimensions.

She told us she could slip out of her body whenever she wanted to. She could enter the larger consciousness system as her true self, not the persona she embodied on earth. When she spoke of visiting fascinating planets and meeting alien beings on her astral journeys, she was as composed as if she were describing a vacation at Myrtle Beach.

Janet explained that we all slipped out of our bodies naturally during sleep, but she wanted to teach us how to do it at will—while awake. She assured us there was nothing to fear, because it was impossible for our souls to permanently detach from our physical bodies. She said they were bound together with a long silvery cord that connected at the solar plexus. She could clearly see her cord whenever she was astrally projected.

She also described how to use mental imagery to place white lights of protection around people we loved, as well as their cars and homes. She said we had the power to prevent some of the accidents that could befall our loved ones or ourselves. Naturally, I found that very comforting.

She guided us in many past life regression meditations. I only glimpsed one of my past lives, though. I saw myself as a young woman dressed in clothing like they wore in the Old West. I was riding a horse, fell off, and landed in a body of water. I'm not sure if I survived that fall, but it was comforting to think that I might have lived before—maybe many times—and I would live again. And so would Lory and Dad.

Again, the twelve weeks zipped by too quickly. Janet wasn't scheduled to teach any more classes at that time, so a couple of other students and I asked her if she'd teach us privately. We knew there was so much more we could learn from her as our spiritual mentor. We were thrilled when she agreed.

Janet welcomed us into her beautiful home every other Saturday afternoon for over two years. We sat on comfortable sofas in her living room, across from a baby grand piano. Several music cases held her favorite guitars. Two Siamese cats skulked around while we sipped Jasmine tea and nibbled popcorn. Sometimes we could hear the laughter of Janet's two young sons as they played outside with their dad. It was heaven.

To help us in our attempts at astral projection, Janet guided us into deep meditations. Then she told us to mentally stand up, and we would pop out of our bodies. We practiced a lot. I don't remember if any of the other students were successful at it, but I never was. Maybe that's because I found out that I was pregnant with our son, and I wasn't comfortable with the idea of leaving my body while there was a baby on board.

But that was okay. It was reassuring to hear Janet say the body and soul were separate entities, and the soul lived on forever after the body died. That way, I could believe that Lory and Dad were beings of energy traveling around the universe instead of just bodies decaying into dust.

I was very fortunate to have Janet as my spiritual teacher for those years. She moved to Michigan, and we lost touch. But I still had the book she gave me. It was called *The Mystic Path to Cosmic Power* by Vernon Howard. She said it summed up the secret to true happiness like no other book she ever read. The author quoted George Gurdjieff, Peter Ouspensky, Walt Whitman, Aldous Huxley, and Plato—those same authors that Grandfather encouraged Paul to read.

Just as Grandfather guided Paul to read, analyze, and absorb what was needed for his spiritual development, Janet helped me to understand how much more of our world there was beyond the obvious. In the years 1981 through 1985, Paul and I had mentors who inspired us to study and learn the secrets of the universe from the very same enlightened thinkers.

CHAPTER NINE

A Touching Bond

Coincidence is God's way of remaining anonymous.

Albert Einstein

When Paul rang my doorbell for our next interview session, I ushered him inside, telling him how fun it was to discover similarities in our lives. He looked dubious, which was understandable. What little I shared with him about my past must have sounded boring and conventional.

"You'll be very surprised when I share those parallels with you, but for now, let's get back to your story," I said as we settled into our usual places on the couch. "When we left off last time your wife, Karyn, moved into town after two years of living with you on the land. You eventually divorced."

"That's correct. But the rest of us lived on the land for two more years. We were healthy, happy, and uplifted by our studies with Grandfather. And in that span of time Cheryl and I married."

"Yes," I said, already knowing that part of his story. "You fell in love with the tough cookie who built her own house. Did your wedding ceremony include the belly dancers again?"

"No." Paul smiled. "We kept things low-key. But soon it became clear that it was time for us to move off the land, and on to whatever life had in store next."

"Oh, how come?" I asked.

"Well, after my divorce from Karyn, it became financially necessary for the trust to sell the land so the proceeds could be divided. But it was okay. In those four years, I'd gotten more out of the experience than I'd ever hoped for. And I knew there were more opportunities for growth awaiting me in the real world. So, it was time to move on.

"When we put the parcel of land up for sale in 1985, a buyer snapped it up right away. So Cheryl, Grandfather, Lisa, and I spent our last few weeks preparing for the changes coming our way. Sarah and Kalima made their own plans, and were ready to set out in new directions. But it was hard to say goodbye to them."

"I can understand that after being so close for four years," I said. "Where did everybody go?"

"I can't remember where Sarah and Kalima were headed at that time. But Cheryl, Copey, and I moved into a modest house we bought in Mancos, Colorado, a half hour outside of Durango. And to thank him for all his teachings and guidance, we provided Grandfather with his own mobile home that sat on a smaller lot adjacent to our property. It was the perfect way for us to continue our studies with him."

"What about Lisa?"

"She moved in with Cheryl and me for a while."

"So, I can't wait to hear. How was it living back in civilization again?"

"Well, it was strange at first. It took time for us to get used to so many people and cars—at least it seemed like a lot to us. Actually, only nine-hundred people lived in Mancos. But the neighborhood screeched with traffic, screaming children, and barking dogs. Cheryl and I felt overwhelmed by all the commotion. We were tempted to jump into our pickup and leave town. We didn't have a plan as to where to go, but a couple of times we actually packed boxes and loaded them onto the truck. But we just couldn't leave. We felt that something was keeping us there, although we didn't know what, yet."

"You mentioned your pickup truck. What happened to your good old VW bus?" I asked.

"It finally died, so we bought a used truck."

"So, how did you finally settle into your new lives?"

"After a while, we just got used to living in the modern world again with its noise, electricity, and indoor plumbing. But we still grew vegetables in our garden, and burned logs in the fireplace for heat. We also continued to get up early for meditations and reading time, studying with Grandfather every day."

"What were you studying at that point?" I asked.

"That was when he guided us in *A Course in Miracles* by Dr. Helen Schucman. The basic tenets included the common thread of acceptance of ourselves and others, forgiveness, and the need to be mindful of our egos in order to realize the joys of pure love. It was a good-sized book—over thirteen hundred pages—that I studied throughout my life.

"Cheryl and I also continued to perform our puppet shows in town. Then we landed jobs running a popular restaurant called Silver Peaks. Cheryl would get to the restaurant at three o'clock every morning to bake a variety of fresh breads. We had a kitchen helper, but we did all the cooking ourselves, using the freshest ingredients we could find. We ordered everything from local distributors or bought from local stores, including meat from the neighborhood butcher shop. It was important to us to support our community. Those were long days, though. I remember staying late every night on cleanup duty."

"Sounds exhausting," I said.

"Yeah, but it was a good experience. After a couple of years we were ready for a change. So we became co-managers of the produce section at our grocery store. We arrived at the store at dawn to set up the displays of fresh fruits and vegetables. We did all the ordering, too. And we created and managed an area of the store where health foods, vitamin and mineral supplements, and organic products were sold. It was the first display of its kind ever seen in Mancos."

"Did you have many customers willing to try those products?" I asked.

"We did. People were becoming more curious about them. So there we were enjoying work, studies, and making improvements to our house. It was a great time. Cheryl even bought a horse and saddle to ride on cattle drives with local cowboys we'd gotten to know at the grocery store."

"Boy, I knew she was tough," I said.

"Yeah it was all good," Paul said, "until back pain hit, radiating down my legs. I'd been working around the yard moving heavy rocks. The pain wasn't so bad at first, but then it grabbed my attention and became constant. I didn't know if I'd pulled a muscle, pinched a nerve or what.

"But I knew I didn't want to see a doctor, a chiropractor, a spiritual healer, a psychic, or anyone else for the pain. I was skeptical of people with degrees, certifications, or letters behind their names, even if their degrees were 'new age' degrees. I knew they'd have their hands out expecting to be paid too much for their services. Besides, I didn't have medical insurance."

"So, what'd you do? Just sit and suffer?"

"I decided to heal the pain myself. I did hours of yoga and stretches. I tried to channel my inner guru and every other spiritual being that I could think of to help me heal. Sometimes the pain did ease for awhile, but it never disappeared for long. It always returned with a vengeance."

"How long did you try to heal yourself?"

"I tried for an entire year, from 1988 to 1989."

"Now that's patience—or extreme stubbornness," I teased.

"Probably some of both," Paul said, "but I was getting desperate for relief by then. That's when people started telling me about some guy named Norman who was a hands-on healer who lived at the top of the hill outside of town. Folks said that the guy worked as a mining engineer at the old Red Arrow mine, but he'd been doing healing work for years. They told me Norman helped them, and he could help my back for sure. They said to just show up at his house because he didn't have a phone."

"What'd you think of that idea?" I asked.

"I took what they said with a grain of salt," Paul said, "but I was very surprised that so many people in that small, conservative town were open-minded about a healer. At that time, alternative and complementary healing methods were practically unheard of.

"And then Copey became seriously ill. That wonderful dog had been a great friend, able to read my thoughts and feelings for fifteen years. I loved him too much to put him through painful medical treatments, so I just let nature take its course. But it was really tough to accept the fact that his life was coming to an end."

"Aw, poor Copey." I said.

"Even though he was weak, he'd somehow muster enough energy to lift his head and wag his tail when I approached. But I knew he was nearing the end when he nipped at me one morning as I tried to stroke his head. All I could do, then, was sit next to him and talk softly. I wasn't surprised, later, when I found his lifeless body under the weeping willow tree in our backyard.

"Cheryl and I wrapped him in a blanket and buried him up in the mountains in his favorite spot. Because of my pain, we moved slowly as we worked the hard ground. We were comforted, though, knowing that Copey would always be in a place that was special to him."

As Paul finished his sentence, I could hear Monty, our thirteen-year-old parrot, chirping and muttering from his cage in the kitchen. That little green-cheeked conure and I had enjoyed a close bond since he was a baby. "That's so sad. I can't imagine the heartbreak someday when I lose Monty," I whispered.

"Yeah. It was a tough time between Copey's death and my constant pain. Cheryl tried every way she could think of to help me. But there was little she could do. I couldn't even sleep most nights. I just tossed and turned in bed, tortured by pain and negative thoughts and questions."

"Like what?" I asked.

"I wondered what I did to deserve so much pain for so long. I just didn't understand it. Why couldn't I heal myself? Then I worried that the pain was a sign I was on the wrong spiritual path. Maybe I wasn't getting better because I wasn't good enough for God or my inner guru. So, in addition to suffering the pain, I questioned my spiritual condition, as well."

"Couldn't Grandfather help you through all that?"

"Whenever Grandfather had medical issues and pain, he just kind of sat back and observed the way his body went through different stages. It didn't matter if he suffered with teeth problems, illnesses, or pain. He simply refused to go to doctors or dentists. But he reminded me that love was all we needed, and that God was within, so I shouldn't be too concerned with the body. He liked to quote from the Shakespeare sonnet, '*Death once dead there is no more dying then.*' Years later at the end of his life, he was having strokes, and he even had a bit of gangrene, too. At that point, he decided it was time, and just let himself die on his own."

"Good heavens," I said. "I don't relish going to doctors or dentists either, but if I ever get to that point, I hope someone will shoot me, or give me enough pain pills so I don't care if I'm literally rotting away. So what finally happened with your back pain?"

Paul's eyes lit up. "One morning after another restless night, I crawled out of bed to run some errands. My first chore was to drive my pickup to the city dump to unload a few bags of trash from the truck bed. But something very strange happened as I was driving."

"Well don't keep me in suspense. What was it?"

"My truck suddenly turned off the main highway, and accelerated up the driveway to the healer's house! It was like being guided by some unseen force. I knew that the healer lived at the top of that hill, but I never made a conscious decision to drive up to see him. I just hung on for the ride until my tires screeched to a stop on a dirt-covered parking area halfway up the hill. From there I saw concrete steps—maybe twenty-five or thirty—leading up to his house."

"It's just like the unseen force that propelled you to the college counselor's office that morning when you were depressed," I interjected.

"It certainly is. See how I've always been guided? When I was looking up at these steps, I suddenly saw three large dogs glaring down at me from the yard at the top of those steps as they paced and barked in unison. Then a man, broad and barrel-chested, appeared behind them. He wore jeans and a tight, white tee shirt. His sleeves were rolled up with a pack of cigarettes in one of them. He had dark hair that was slicked back into a pompadour. He looked like he just stepped out of the musical *Grease*."

"You're kidding," I said with a snort." So, what'd you do?"

"I waved up at him and said I was looking for Norman, the guy who did healing work. When he said he was Norman, I was shocked. I wasn't expecting the healer to be some average looking dude with an Elvis hairdo."

"What were you expecting him to look like?"

"Someone more spiritual looking—maybe with beads, a beard, or a long robe. But I figured I had nothing to lose, so I told him I needed help with back pain. He smiled then, and even from that distance, I could see he was missing some teeth. He told me to come up to the house, as he shooed his dogs away.

"I slowly made my way up all those steps, wondering how other injured or sick people managed it. When I got to the top, I followed Norman through a set of sliding glass doors into his house. Suddenly I was engulfed in a thick cloud of cigarette smoke. Even though my parents had smoked in our house growing up, I'd never seen a room that hazy. My eyes watered as I tried to see through the mist."

I drew in a deep breath. "It must have been suffocating in there."

"It was pretty bad at first, but it improved after a while, or maybe I got used to it. As we walked into the kitchen, a woman was pouring fresh-brewed coffee into a cup. She was slim, wearing tight blue jeans and a thin sweater. A lit cigarette was dangling from her lips, its smoke causing one of her heavily made-up eyes to squint. Her short frosted hair was sprayed stiffly into place."

I chuckled. "Well, that is some description. Too bad I can't tell if she was attractive or hideous."

"Oh, she was attractive," Paul said. "Norman introduced her as his wife, Carole. He said that Carole also gave healing sessions to people. Then he explained that they were heavy coffee drinkers, so a fresh pot of coffee brewed in their kitchen daily from six in the morning until midnight."

"Now that's what I'd call a serious caffeine habit."

"I'll say. Carole poured me a cup and invited me to join them at their table for a morning snack. As we sat there, she put a plate in front of me that was piled high with a variety of cookies. Norman boasted that he and Carole ate a typical American diet of red meat and white bread. He said they avoided healthy foods such as tofu, brown rice, and broccoli like the plague. As I munched, I watched them eat cookies, drink coffee, and smoke cigarettes, lighting fresh ones immediately after stubbing out the old ones. The ashtrays around the room were filled with butts. I was flabbergasted . . . healers who enjoyed coffee, cookies and cigarettes? Unheard of!

"We talked a while, then Norman told me to follow him into the master bedroom. Once inside, he asked me to sit on the edge of the bed and remove my shirt. He disappeared for a moment, and I could hear him washing his hands in the adjoining bathroom. Then he came close, touching lightly on the skin under my breastbone area, and then behind my neck. He said that was the greeting, similar to starting a car's engine by turning the key. Next, he touched different areas around my body before having me turn face-down on the bed so that he could touch points along my back."

"How were you feeling during that experience?" I asked.

"I remember thinking how strange it was. I couldn't imagine how such light touching—although certainly pleasant—could ever alleviate my pain. I had no idea how much time had passed, when Norman suddenly left the room. I wasn't sure if he was even finished or not, so I continued to lie on the bed, enjoying how relaxed I felt.

"But after a few minutes I assumed he was done. I stood up, put my shirt on, and made my way back to the kitchen. Carole and Norman were relaxing at the table, sipping more coffee, with lit cigarettes between their fingers. I couldn't contain my curiosity, so I asked Norman what exactly he did to me. He said he just touched me. But when I asked him where he got the technique, he waved me off saying that it just came to him one day. Then he asked how I was feeling.

"That's when I realized how much looser my body felt. I could easily grab my wallet out of my back pocket. I told him I felt a little better already, and asked how much I owed him. Norman shook his head, saying that he and Carole didn't charge people for their services. I was astounded."

"Didn't the people in town tell you that Norman's healings were free?" I asked.

"No. They hadn't mentioned it, and I was so desperate to be rid of the pain, I never asked them. Well, after Norman told me he didn't charge, I managed to mumble a thank you to them and hurried down the steps to my truck. I couldn't wrap my brain around the fact that they didn't charge for their healings and didn't have their hands out for payment like other healers. I'd always felt strongly that healers shouldn't charge. It just never seemed right to me.

"I was already stunned by the down-to-earth way Norman and Carole ate, dressed, and spoke, with no pretense at being all-knowing gurus. They certainly weren't the stereotypical healers who used meditation gongs, singing bowls, or incense burners. I even saw a small arsenal of firearms in their gun cabinet. Norman noticed me looking at it, and matter-of-factly explained that the guns were strictly for the pleasure of hunting and killing game.

"I reached my truck, easily sliding behind the wheel," Paul continued. "As I coasted down the hill, I compared Norman's way of life to my own vegetarian, passive way of living. I believed in non-violent resistance—that all forms of life were sacred and shouldn't be killed—even for my own survival. I'd just assumed that was a necessary philosophy to live by to lead a spiritual life. But that theory had just been blown out of the water! I just met a man who was a gifted healer despite the fact that he killed animals for sport and ate their meat."

"So what did that tell you?" I asked. "What did it mean?"

"I asked myself that same question. I thought about all of my years of strict disciplines, philosophical studies, and shunning society in order to immerse myself in a truly spiritual life. And now I wondered if all that had really been necessary in order to attain my spiritual goals. And as I dropped the trash at the dump, I was amazed at how easily I could handle the bags without pain. I drove home, anxious to tell Cheryl about my experience."

"You already noticed a difference in the amount of pain you were feeling?"

"Oh yes. It was significantly reduced," he answered. "Cheryl was so happy to hear my story, and relieved to see excitement on my face instead of pain. I took her up the hill to meet Norman and Carole the next day, and she was as fascinated by them as I was. Soon we were spending a lot of time there."

"Why? What did you do there?" I asked.

"We sat with people who were waiting to have healing sessions. We listened to their stories. At any given time, there were at least four or five of them sitting in the kitchen or living room, waiting their turns. Most smoked cigarettes, drank coffee, and ate cookies. Norman and Carole didn't have a telephone, so people couldn't call for a specific appointment time. As they showed up, they simply wrote their names on a piece of paper that served as the schedule. Norman and Carole each took one person at a time into a bedroom for a session.

"Cheryl and I were surprised by the diversity of the people who waited there, everyone from Mormons and Baptists to ranchers and Indians from the nearby reservations. There were some lively conversations going on, believe me. Then after their sessions, people often sat back down in the living room to continue chatting and snacking. Folks came and went throughout the day, from morning 'til dinner time, and sometimes even into the evening. Many of them brought donations of coffee, cookies, cigarettes, groceries, or small amounts of money that they would hide, so that Norman and Carole wouldn't happen upon them until later. In that way, those donations would be accepted. Carole once told me she didn't need to buy coffee for years because she found so many cans hidden under the beds. She said someone even hid dollar bills under the toilet seat.

"Some evenings Norman and Carole looked very tired from the long days. I'm sure they were relieved to see everyone go home. But if anyone showed up at their door, even in the middle of the night, Norman got out of bed to give them a session while Carole brewed fresh coffee."

"That's incredible devotion." I said. "What big-hearted people. In the meantime, how was your back doing?"

"My pain completely vanished after only two sessions with Norman! And with maintenance sessions for six months afterwards, my entire body corrected and adjusted as if creating a whole new structure. My back realigned itself, and I actually grew an inch as my spine straightened."

"Wow. Well no wonder you were so amazed by it," I said.

"I couldn't believe getting that kind of result from a simple touch technique. I began to think that maybe it was fate. Maybe I was meant to suffer—according to some Divine plan—in order to meet Norman and Carole and embrace their healing technique."

I nodded in agreement. "It sure sounds like it."

"So," Paul continued, "Cheryl and I spent more and more time at Norman and Carole's house, talking to people. One day a tall, muscular rancher told us that when he first came to Norman, his arm was badly injured. The arm muscle had atrophied so much he could fit his other fist into where he used to have the muscle. But after a few weeks of sessions, his muscle started to rebuild, and eventually returned to normal in appearance and strength.

"Another day, a woman told us how an excruciating case of shingles drove her to consider suicide before she finally sought help from Norman. She said that when Norman worked on her, it was the first time she could withstand anyone touching her in months. Within a few sessions, her pain had completely disappeared. She had tears in her eyes as she talked about the miracle she received at that house, and how she continued with regular sessions to make sure she stayed healthy.

"As that lady finished talking, I heard Norman's dogs barking, announcing someone else's arrival. I looked out the window to see a man with an oxygen tank struggling to climb up the steps to the house. Frank, a truck driver I'd known for years, had a heart condition which caused shortness of breath. When he finally made it to the living room, he said it was his first time there. He slowly followed Norman into a bedroom. After the session, I laughed as Frank waved goodbye to me, briskly walking out of the house. He'd forgotten to take his oxygen tank with him!"

"That's incredible," I said, "but why in the world would healers live in a house with so many steps for people to climb?"

"I don't know why they bought that particular house, but I always compared it to the pilgrimage up Rome's Holy Staircase in Christian tradition. If you wanted to be healed, you had to make it up those steps," Paul stressed. "I vividly remember a high school football player who broke his ankle during a game. The teenager went to his doctor, who wanted to put him in a cast. But having heard about Norman's healing technique, the boy asked his doctor to put a temporary cast on his ankle instead. That way, he could take it off and put it on by himself whenever he wanted to. That kid's determination amazed me, because every day after school, he hobbled up the steps, took off his cast, and Norman or Carole worked on him. Within a few weeks, his doctor was dumbfounded at how quickly that ankle healed. And not long after that, I had an epiphany."

"Well, you hadn't had one in a while," I teased. "Tell about this one."

"Cheryl and I were hanging out in Norman's living room, when people started gossiping about two local feuding families. Apparently, the people involved had never gotten along, in a way similar to the Hatfield–McCoy conflict. Members of the clans lived in the general vicinity, but had avoided each other for decades to prevent bloodshed. Yet everyone was bewildered because whenever any of those family members happened to show up at Norman's at the same time, they were able to sit together, peacefully, waiting their turn. Suddenly an elderly rancher who'd been sitting with us got to his feet. He was one of the town's old timers. He looked at us and said, 'You wanna know why those feuding clan members can sit together peacefully in this living room? It's because Norman and Carole brought love here. And people can feel it. Yep, Norman and Carole brought love to Mancos Valley!'

"Well, his words sent a shiver through me," Paul continued. "Then I heard 'Aha' booming in my head. I immediately thought of the people in the world who were suffering, feeling alone and afraid—the common denominator of all humanity. But Norman's healing method eliminated pain, provided a sense of well-being, and delivered a form of love that people desperately needed. I couldn't imagine a better application of 'love thy neighbor' than that!"

"Now that was a good epiphany," I said.

"Later that evening, when Cheryl and I were alone with Norman and Carole, I took the opportunity to ask Norman where he had gotten the healing technique. I asked once before, but he ducked the question. This time, he could see I was determined to hear the truth. He took a deep breath and started talking.

"He said that back in 1973, he and Carole were living in Quartzsite, Arizona, where he worked as a mining engineer. He was having a beer at his friend John's house one night when John's young son ran into the room screaming that his mother was bleeding again. John's wife, four months pregnant, was losing blood just as she had during two previous miscarriages. John jumped to his feet, panicking. Suddenly, Norman knew what to do. He told John that he felt certain he could help his wife if he could touch her for a few minutes. John looked confused, but said okay. He was open to anything at that point.

"The wife was lying on the bed crying. Norman told her that he could help if she would allow him to touch her around her abdomen. She nodded, so he lightly pressed on points around her mid section. He said that the knowledge of how and where to touch her just came to him . . . from somewhere he didn't even know. But he didn't question it; he just followed the inner guidance. And after he touched her for about twenty minutes, her painful cramps eased, and a short time later, the bleeding slowed to a stop. She eventually carried that baby to full term, giving birth to a healthy boy."

"It's inconceivable how the knowledge just came to him like that. Did you believe that story?" I asked.

"Yes," Paul answered. "Carole said that when Norman came home from John's house that night, and told her what happened, she peppered him with questions. She wondered how he knew what to do without having any medical training. She asked if he heard voices giving him instructions. She needed to understand. But he had no answers for her. He said he had no idea how he knew what to do. He just knew. Then he admitted that he was content not knowing how or why. He was going to simply accept the fact that—for some reason—he received that knowledge. So, she had to accept it too."

"But that doesn't really explain the origin of the technique, does it? I mean, isn't it weird to have no idea where it actually came from?" I insisted.

"That's the mystique of Bio-Touch. We don't know where it came from or why it works. We just have to accept it. That's what makes it so perfect." Paul's face beamed.

"Okay, but I would still love to know. So continue with Norman's story."

"Well, people heard what Norman had done to help John's wife, so they started showing up at his door asking for healings for themselves. Norman touched specific points on their bodies—wherever he felt drawn to do so—and they felt better. Soon, he noticed a pattern emerging. For instance, when he worked on people with headaches, Norman found himself touching the same points on the back of each person's neck. When people had sinus problems, he touched the exact same points on each of their faces. So, he began to write down precisely where those points could be found on the body, and what conditions he was using them for.

"But after a while, Norman became overwhelmed by the amount of people seeking his help, so he decided to teach Carole the technique. He was curious to see if someone else would be effective using it. And sure enough after learning the points, she was just as proficient at using his healing method as he was.

"When I heard that part of Norman's story, I got very excited," Paul said. "I realized that people all over the world could learn how to share the technique. It wasn't just for Norman and Carole, or for some gifted healers. It was for everyone. So, I asked Norman and Carole if they would teach Cheryl and me how to do it. They agreed. And after we learned the points, we gave people sessions, too, which allowed Norman and Carole to enjoy some down time."

"You must have been thrilled to finally find something so special to devote your life to," I said.

"Well, I had a rather rocky beginning. You see, one day Norman received a letter from the parents of a nine year old boy named Kevin. Kevin had suffered from cancer for four years, enduring medical treatments that included high doses of chemotherapy. There was nothing more the doctors could do for his leukemia, so he had just been sent home from the hospital to die.

"The parents heard about Norman's healing work. They weren't able to call since Norman didn't have a phone, so they wrote, begging him to fly to their home in Corpus Christi, Texas to help their son. They even included a check to cover the cost of round trip airfare. Touched by their crisis, Norman, Carole, Cheryl, and I discussed what to do. We agreed that I'd fly to Texas right away."

"But how did the parents hear about Norman?" I asked. "Researching such things on the Internet wasn't available yet."

"I'm not sure how they heard about him," Paul answered, "but it was probably through the grapevine. Someone in Mancos must have known that family, and when I arrived at their home, I explained to the parents that I'd been sent in Norman's place.

"They thanked me for coming and led me to their master bedroom, which was set up like a hospital room. A large railed bed took up most of the area. Kevin was asleep in the bed, an oxygen mask covering his nose and mouth. His small body was just skin and bones. He seemed to be going in and out of consciousness.

"I hesitated a moment before touching him. I'd only been giving healing sessions for a few months, so I was nervous to work on such a frail child. But once I began, I relaxed. Kevin stirred slightly during the session, but never opened his eyes.

"Afterwards, Kevin's father and I ate a snack in the living room. I heard Kevin's mother getting something in the kitchen. Soon she returned to the living room with an ecstatic look on her face. She said Kevin had seemed restless, so she offered him some pudding. He hadn't eaten any solid food for over a week, but he licked the spoon, seemed to want more, and wound up eating five spoonfuls.

"Hearing that, Kevin's father jumped up and ran to be with his son. The mother joined him, while I stayed on the couch, giving them privacy. They came back to the living room with smiles on their faces. They said Kevin was sleeping again, but he seemed calm and peaceful. Then they thanked me, saying they knew the healing session had already helped him.

"They talked for hours about Kevin. Their faces lit up as they described how he was the kind of child who never complained, even though he was seriously ill. They told me how people—even strangers—could see and feel his love and concern for others. Then when he got sick, their friends, family, and neighbors rallied together, collecting money and organizing fundraisers to help defray the cost of his medical treatments. They shared their stories with me until two in the morning.

"I went into the guest room, while the parents joined Kevin in his bed, sleeping on either side of him, as they usually did. Tossing and turning, I finally fell into an uneasy sleep, when I was scared awake by a loud hissing noise coming from their bedroom. It sounded like oxygen was escaping from Kevin's tank.

"Then I heard crying and shouting. ' Paul! Come quick! Kevin's not breathing!'

"My heart pounded as I jumped out of bed and dashed into their room. Kevin's mother was kneeling on the bed, sobbing and cradling her son in her arms. She kept begging him to wake up. Kevin's dad was holding the phone frantically calling for an ambulance. I immediately started another session on Kevin, but I knew it was too late. It looked like he'd been gone for a while.

"The paramedics arrived quickly, and Kevin was rushed to the hospital. His parents followed in the car. I stayed in their house for the remainder of the night, pacing the floor, and feeling sick to my stomach. Kevin's parents had been so happy because he'd eaten some pudding. And now he was dead. That session I gave him hadn't helped at all. I'd failed the child and his family.

"A while later, a man knocked at the door. With tears in his eyes, he told me that he was a neighbor, and that Kevin had, indeed, passed away. His parents had asked the man to let me know. Distraught, I thanked the neighbor and scribbled a note of condolence to them. Then I called a taxi to take me back to the airport. I didn't want to be there, intruding, when they returned in mourning."

"Oh, how horrible," I said as I shook my head. "That was a weighty responsibility on your shoulders so soon after you'd learned the technique. How'd you handle it?"

"Not well," Paul admitted. "When I got home, I didn't leave my house for over a week. I was grief-stricken, questioning myself as well as the effectiveness of the healing method. Cheryl and Grandfather tried to console me, but nothing they said made me feel better. Norman and Carole came to visit, explaining that when it was someone's time to die—even a child's—the healing method could ease symptoms, but not stop the inevitable. But I didn't want to hear it.

"And then they showed me a letter they had received from Kevin's mother. She wrote that since things had quieted down after the funeral, she could take the time to thank me. I couldn't believe my eyes when I read how grateful she and her husband were for my visit and the healing session I gave Kevin. They knew, because of that session, that their son was able to enjoy his last meal and pass away peacefully. He was able to stop fighting, and could finally let go. He'd been struggling against the disease for so long. But that session helped him realize that it was okay, that he didn't have to fight anymore. The session I had with him helped Kevin understand that."

My throat tightened as chills raced up and down my arms. "How'd it make you feel to read that?" I whispered.

"Tremendously relieved," Paul answered. "And that's the moment I knew I could dedicate the rest of my life to that loving way of touching others—even those who couldn't be cured.

"Later that day, I walked over to Grandfather's house. He met me at the door with a cup of coffee, and we sat quietly for a while. Grandfather knew Cheryl and I had observed the healing technique for over nine months, and practiced it for a few months more. I'd previously told him how effective it was on everybody—people of all backgrounds, all levels of education, all ages, all beliefs, and all attitudes. I even told him how I saw it help a few people who didn't want it to work, they were so ornery. And then I told him about the letter from Kevin's mother, and how the technique had allowed a small, ill child to let go and pass away.

"I told him that I was ready to get more involved—that it was time for me to share the technique with as many people as possible. But my concern was whether it would interfere with the path I'd been on for so long, to diminish the power of my ego. I looked at my mentor and asked him if he thought my ego would grow if I got involved. I needed him to reassure me that my ego wouldn't expand every time I helped someone heal.

"Grandfather's black eyes sparkled. 'If you don't get involved, Paul, that's your ego.'

"And that was the defining moment for me!" Paul exclaimed, getting to his feet. "My only doubt had been put to rest. I was free to share that healing method with anyone who needed it. That meant Cheryl and I could practice the principles of 'love thy neighbor as thyself' and the Golden Rule without having to preach them. Therefore, it wouldn't be just about healing bodies, but also about living those important philosophies, too. It was perfect." He picked up his water bottle and keys signaling that the session was over for the day.

As I walked him to the door, I shook my head.

"What?" he asked.

"I already know the parallel in our lives for the period we just covered, from the years 1985 to 1989," I said.

"Really? What is it?" he asked.

"I'll tell you soon. Better yet, I'll let you read it for yourself when I'm done writing it."

"Okay, okay." He laughed as he walked to his car.

I closed the door, and made my way to the kitchen. As I busied myself peeling potatoes, carrots, and onions to add to the simmering pot roast, it occurred to me that the similarity in our lives for those years was the most profound of all. We were both using our hands to help people feel better. While Paul was learning and sharing Norman's healing method, I was studying hands-on healing books and practicing on any friends and family members who'd allow me to.

After seeing the movie *Resurrection,* in 1980, I knew I wanted to touch and heal people. I explored a different path for a while studying spiritual concepts with my teacher, Janet. But when she moved away, my desire to touch people returned full force.

I wasn't nearly as effective as Paul, even though we were both beginners. While he helped people right off the bat, I was happy if folks could actually tell I'd worked on them. Of course, that was because I hadn't discovered the right healing technique, yet. The important thing though, was how, at the same time, we both chose to help ease people's pain and suffering in the most loving way—by touching them. So, what to make of all the coincidences in our lives?

The online site, *Urban Dictionary,* has a definition of kindred spirits as "two people that make a special connection by sharing a bond that has joined them together, through their experiences, on a higher level of consciousness. This connection can be from the same experience at the same time or separate experiences similar in nature."

Was it possible that Paul and I were kindred spirits? I didn't know, but maybe that's why I considered him to be the brother I never had. He was fun to joke and laugh with. When we teased each other, there was a warm familiarity between us. Like any brother, he found things to bug me about—like my sleep cycle. He couldn't believe it when he heard I was a night owl, writing well past midnight, then sleeping until ten or ten thirty in the morning. That was a slothful concept to him, so he took every opportunity to tell me so.

He also made fun of my clean-freak tendencies. He said he tried, but couldn't find a single speck of dust in my house. And according to him, I bathed too often, because I was petrified of being natural or—heaven forbid—getting dirty. I couldn't disagree with him. I was just so glad he never saw inside our master bathroom cabinets; I never would have heard the end of it. He would have flipped seeing the profusion of my lotions, potions, perfumes, and cosmetics. But he would have teased me most unmercifully if he had seen my collection of soaps. Bar soaps, my guilty pleasure. I could never resist picking up a gorgeous, luscious one. Many were given to me as gifts, and were too special to ever use. Those included the large neon-yellow lemon soaps that Jill brought back each time she visited Sorrento, Italy.

Whenever Howard spotted homemade soaps at craft fairs, he bought several bars in different hues and shapes, further fueling my addiction. I loved looking at and sniffing the amber-colored sandalwood rectangles, hot-pink rose-scented hearts, strawberry-glycerin wedges, French vanilla ovals with flecks of oatmeal, and minty ice-blue swans that graced our bathroom with their aromatic beauty. Sometimes I even washed with them.

But getting back to Paul, I liked his serious side, too. He was an attentive listener. He always had time to hear my thoughts and answer questions, sharing his philosophical and spiritual insights, which I trusted and respected. He offered solid brotherly advice whenever I needed it. His perspective was refreshing, and he was usually so spot on about things, it was uncanny.

However, Paul and I sometimes annoyed the hell out of each other, as any siblings might do. We even got into a fight, once. We were both so furious, we could have bitten off each other's heads. We were at the Bio-Touch Center on a sweltering summer afternoon. Another practitioner was working that day, too. We were each in a room, giving sessions to our recipients. As always, I was warm, but that day, the room felt even hotter than usual. My recipient sweated right along with me.

Suddenly, an intensely itchy heat rash erupted across my back and abdomen. Prickly heat! It was something I had suffered from since childhood. For some reason, I never outgrew it, like most people did. Whenever I got over-heated to the point of perspiring, those tiny tickly bumps emerged. The urgency to scratch at myself superseded everything else. I knew that the solution was as simple as cooling myself down or, better yet, avoiding sweating in the first place.

I had never told Paul or the other practitioners about my rash. They already knew I grew too hot during sessions, but I was too embarrassed to admit I suffered from prickly heat. Besides, I didn't want Paul to have something else to tease me about. I could almost hear him laughing that I was allergic to my own sweat.

I asked my recipient to excuse me, left the session room, and walked over to the thermostat located on the wall. When I turned it down one degree, I could hear the air-conditioner kick on. Knowing relief would come soon, I resumed giving the session. Then, just when it started to feel cooler, I heard the air-conditioner click off again. Soon the air hung humid and heavy in the stifling room. I scratched at my skin.

Excusing myself for a second time, I went back to the thermostat. Someone had turned it up, so I turned it down once more before returning to my recipient. But again, the cool air shut off right away. I couldn't believe my eyes when I went to look at the thermostat a third time. There was a little sign taped over it that read "LEAVE ALONE." I recognized Paul's handwriting. I didn't want to be pushy, but I couldn't leave the thermostat alone. I was too miserable. So I slid my finger under the sign, turned the temperature down a degree, and went back to finish the session while the cool air was blowing.

Afterwards, I walked to the sink to wash my hands. Paul was waiting there for me. His mouth was a tight, thin line; his eyes were darkening storm clouds. He blurted out how angry he was that I had ignored his sign, and how the center didn't revolve around me and my comfort. Then he informed me that he and his recipient, and the other practitioner were way too cold, that they would need mittens soon. As he berated me for being inconsiderate to others, his head bobbed like a pigeon's, punctuating each clipped word.

I was shocked at how livid he was. I tried to lighten his mood by joking that he and the others were too skinny, and needed to have more body fat like I had in order to stay warm. But he wasn't having it. His expression remained harsh.

I told him that I only turned the thermostat down one degree, just to get it to click on. There was no way that one degree could have taken the temperature from Mohave Desert to North Pole. But he loudly insisted that the one degree caused everyone else to freeze. It stung to be the object of his fury. I had seen Paul annoyed with people at the center before, but he never raised his voice to them. In fact, I was impressed at how patient, calm, and respectful he always was with everyone. So why wasn't he being like that with me? I cringed knowing others could hear him reprimanding me.

White-hot fury exploded inside me. Rising onto my tiptoes, I lifted my face toward his, and demanded that we go outside to discuss the matter privately. He agreed, shrugging his shoulders. Once we were on the back patio, I stood glowering, dying to tell him to go screw himself. He had no right to scold me like I was a naughty child, or blow my "crime" so far out of proportion. I wanted to get away from him; I needed to put as much distance between me and his cold eyes as possible.

But instead of running away, I forced my feet to stay where they were because I knew my next recipient was waiting for me. I turned away from Paul, more comfortable looking at the parking lot, than his face. Then I admitted my heat rash issue. A few tears dared to slide down my cheeks as I spoke. I resented having to tell him, but I felt pressured to explain my misbehavior with the thermostat.

As he listened, the anger evaporated from his face. After a few moments, he said he appreciated my candor and wished I had confided in him about it sooner. The warmth returned to his voice as he reminded me that Bio-Touch could certainly help my problem. Then he explained that the session room I was working in was the hottest in the building, so I should move to a different one. He also said he was sure we could work out a way to keep me comfortable while I gave sessions in the future.

I stood silently staring at the parked cars with my arms crossed. Paul said some more things in a friendly tone, but I barely heard him. When he went back inside the building, I realized I was shaking. There was a pain in my midsection that felt like someone punched me. My lungs were so heavy, it was hard to draw in deep breaths. It took every last bit of strength to drag myself back inside and act like everything was normal in front of my recipient.

A few days later I received an email from Paul saying that he felt bad about the incident. It didn't sound like much of an apology, but I wrote back something vague about feeling bad about it too. The truth was I wasn't ready to forgive him. In fact, I held a grudge for weeks. Whenever we were together at the center, I avoided conversation with him, barely able to tolerate being in the same room. I was still hurt and angry. For some reason, I had really pushed his buttons that day, and he over-reacted. I didn't understand why. Maybe he was having a lousy day. He was human, after all, but I just couldn't let it go.

Howard felt bad about our fight. He said I was wrong to keep changing the thermostat without explanation, but Paul was wrong to fly off the handle like he did. He suggested I have an honest conversation with Paul, letting him know how I felt. I knew my husband was right, but I wasn't ready to admit to Paul how much he hurt my feelings.

I confided in Nobu, one of the other practitioners, about what happened. She explained that she'd known Paul for a long time and knew what a good man he was. She said he must have felt extremely close to me to be able to reveal his true feelings . . . trusting me with his unvarnished anger.

I was shocked by her words. I hadn't thought of it that way at all. I figured that he didn't feel close to me, which was why he lost his temper. But now I could see that she was right. I thought of the times I had unleashed my anger at safe targets. Those people loved me, and I knew they would still be there for me after my rant was over. If that was how Paul was feeling, it changed everything. It meant I was a safe target for him. And as long as I wasn't a target very often, everything would be fine.

I also realized that I was furious with him because I thought he was frivolously withdrawing his friendship over something petty. Apparently, I still had fear around the sudden loss, perceived or real, of a close relationship. It scared me to think my brother-figure could so easily sever our kinship.

With my newly found insight, my friendship with Paul quickly resumed its former harmony. I was able to put the whole thing behind me. In fact, it wasn't until a year later that we finally talked about it with a calm clarity aided by the passage of time. But in the meantime, he accommodated me whenever I needed to lower the thermostat at the center. Extra fans were set up in the session rooms, and I began to wear a cooling neck-wrap during sessions, as well.

So, are Paul and I kindred spirits? His destiny led him to Bio-Touch, and eventually, to Tucson. My destiny led me to Tucson, and eventually to Bio-Touch. Over the span of four decades, our lives were peppered again and again, with similar experiences happening at the exact same time. My relationship with him is the closest I've known to having a brother. He calls me "sister." I don't know if Paul and I are soul-siblings, but I know how fascinating it is to contemplate the possibility.

Debra Schildhouse and Paul Bucky in Tucson, Arizona, in May 2015

Photo by Jennifer Vimmerstedt

CHAPTER TEN

Bio-Touch is Born

There is no better way to thank God for your sight than by
giving a helping hand to someone in the dark.

Helen Keller

Light in My Darkness

When I saw Paul again I said, "At the end of last week's interview you realized you were ready to jump in with both feet—to really get involved in the healing technique. You had Cheryl's support and Grandfather's blessing. What did you do next?"

Paul settled himself comfortably on the couch. "Well, Norman and Carole mentioned that they wanted to move to Oregon someday," he answered. "They dreamed of setting up a training center there to teach people the healing technique. But I couldn't see the point in waiting until someday to do it; I was anxious to get started. I asked if they would let Cheryl and me help them start teaching right away.

"Carole smiled at me as she shook her head. She said that when she first met me in her kitchen almost a year before, she wondered who that hippie was and what he wanted. Now she knew. She said I obviously came into their lives to be their 'noodge'—to goad them into starting their training center earlier than they'd planned.

"So we got busy transforming their basement into a classroom. After the cleaning and straightening was done, we set up folding chairs in a semi-circle configuration. We placed a life-sized female mannequin in the middle of it. We hoped that pointing out the precise touch points on the old donated dummy would be an effective way to teach the students."

"And of course it was," I said. I chuckled remembering how relieved I was that the weird, draped mannequin had a legitimate purpose.

"Yeah, it turned out to be a great visual aid," Paul agreed. "Meanwhile, Norman and I poured over all his notes about touch points on the body, and created our first crudely made training manual. We then told everyone we knew where and when the first Bio-Touch training class would be held."

"Did you get many students?"

"Yes. We had twenty show up to that first class in the fall of 1989. That class was mostly made up of people who had regular sessions with Norman and Carole. They were excited to participate in our very first class."

"One of those first students, a local businessman, was so impressed with the healing technique, he said he wanted to help our effort. He spent hours helping me create a clearly written manual with pictures. He also offered the use of his office, his word processor, and his small printing press for printing a few dozen copies of that first manual."

"Did the technique have an official name, yet?" I asked.

"Norman thought it should be called Bio-Magnetic Touch Healing."

"Why did he like that particular name? There's no use of magnets."

"I think he chose the words Bio-Magnetic because of research that was done regarding the electromagnetic field in and around the body. Albert Roy Davis and Walter C. Rawls Jr. used the term in their book *Magnetism and its Effects on the Living System.* The word 'Bio' refers to the living body and 'Magnetic' refers to the energy field surrounding us. For him, that name aptly described the healing technique. Our first manuals were printed using that name on the cover. Of course years later we shortened the name to Bio-Touch, which would eventually become our trademarked name."

"That was a smart move. That other name had too many syllables," I said.

"And as luck would have it," Paul continued, "another one of our students happened to be a lawyer. He was so inspired by the class, he volunteered to help me create a nonprofit organization for the teaching of Bio-Touch. Soon I was signing corporate papers and becoming educated about nonprofit development. Me—the guy who dropped out of society and hated organizations," he said, laughing. "But Cheryl and I loved the idea of creating an educational foundation to encourage people to grow in their own self-awareness. It wasn't set up to be a foundation for healing, but a way to apply the principle 'love thy neighbor' while teaching people to help others as well as themselves.

"And there was one more student who wanted to help us. He was a Certified Public Accountant who helped me create a tax-exempt organization.

"The Internal Revenue Code allows for federal tax exemption of nonprofit organizations, specifically those that are considered public charities or, as in our case, educational foundations. It's a process that normally takes from one to three years to complete. So we couldn't believe it when only ninety days after we applied, a letter arrived confirming that our new organization had been given tax exempt status by the IRS. Things were falling into place so easily we just knew it was meant to be.

"So, Norman, Carole, Cheryl, and I became the founding Board of Directors. We taught classes regularly in our training center and continued to give people healing sessions upstairs. But it soon became clear that we needed more space to accommodate our growing number of recipients. We needed a larger dedicated area to allow students to practice their skills toward completing our newly formed practitioner training and certification programs.

"Cheryl and I bought an inexpensive mobile home right down the street from our house. The place was small, maybe twelve by forty feet, but it was situated on a heavily treed lot. And it had two nice-sized bedrooms to use as session rooms. Friends helped us build a ramp up to the front porch to accommodate wheelchairs. We put chairs in the living room, which served as the waiting area. And on a small table in the kitchen were plates of cookies, along with a coffee-maker and tea-pot that brewed all day.

"It was the first official Bio-Touch Center. And it quickly became a busy place, too. Cheryl and I, and our new practitioners, gave sessions to recipients every day. Volunteers helped with the day-to-day management of the place. People could now call and make appointments.

"Sounds a lot like our present-day center," I remarked.

"Exactly," Paul said. "There was an elderly man, named Tom, who lived next door to the center. He had a reputation for being cranky—probably due to his chronic pain from an old back injury. He would sit on his porch and glare at everybody coming in and out of the center. One day I invited him to come inside. I explained what Bio-Touch was, but he declined, saying he didn't believe in such things. When I told him there was no charge, so he had nothing to lose, he agreed to have a session. After that, Tom showed up two or three times a week for a month. He was still dubious, even as his pain lessened. But he was less grumpy.

"Imagine our shock when he burst through the center door one day, smiling from ear to ear. He said he wanted us to see what he could do. He jumped high into the air, clicking his heels together. I can still see the triumphant look on his face. He announced that he had absolutely no pain. He said he'd been holding his chainsaw, cutting wood for hours—something he hadn't been able to do in years. Then he thanked us with tears in his eyes."

"Well, you sure pulled the thorn out of that lion's paw," I chuckled, making reference to my favorite Aesop's fable.

"Yeah, he was a new man," Paul said.

"And what were Norman and Carole doing while all this was going on?" I asked.

"They were still giving healing sessions at their house. But they sent their overflow recipients to the center. They visited regularly, watching the action, and supervising new practitioners," Paul answered. "So, here's a story for you. One night I was alone at the center finishing some paperwork. As I got ready to walk home, I opened the front door, stepped onto the dark porch, and turned to lock the door. I heard a rustling sound behind me, and I whirled around to see a man and a woman standing in the shadows. They were Native-Americans. The woman held an infant wrapped in a thick wool blanket. I asked how I could help them, and in broken English, they explained that they lived on the nearby reservation and needed a healing session for their baby. They were worried because the child was having frequent seizures that not only interrupted his sleep, but made it impossible for them to sleep, as well. They were all miserable.

"They went on to say that they came to the center because of a relative's recommendation. He told them that there was no charge for our healing services. They were desperate for help, but couldn't afford to pay their own medicine man."

"Wait a minute," I interrupted. "They had to pay for the services of their medicine man? I'd always assumed that tribe members automatically had free access to their medicine man."

"Apparently, not in this case," Paul replied. "Anyway, I invited the couple inside. I was pretty nervous as I laid the baby on one of the beds. He was very young, and obviously very sick. I worried that their medicine man would hold me responsible if the child got sicker, or even died. But I had to erase those fears from my mind. I touched the tiny boy, but he had a seizure right away! I was ready to freak out," Paul said, as his eyes widened.

"Oh, that would be terrifying," I said with a gulp.

"It was. But I forced myself to calm down. I just kept touching the child on the stress points, while I figured out what else to do." Paul's fingers traced imaginary points in the air. "When I worked on his head for a while, his seizures finally stopped. I was so relieved. The baby seemed relaxed as his mother lifted him from the bed. But I worried about him for weeks after they left. I prayed that the boy was better. I also hoped like hell I wouldn't be visited by their angry medicine man."

"I'll bet," I said laughing. "So, what happened?"

"About a month later, I was giving a session to a Native-American man who'd been coming to the center regularly for months. While I worked on him, he casually mentioned that his sister and her husband had visited me with their sick baby one night. I told him how much I'd been worrying about that child and asked how he was doing. The man said that after I gave his little nephew that session, the child slept through the night for the first time in his life. The baby was no longer having seizures, either. The family was thrilled and very grateful to finally be getting some sleep."

"Well how nice of the uncle to finally get around to telling you," I said. "You must have been so relieved."

"Yeah, not only was it great to hear that the little guy was doing well, but then I could stop looking over my shoulder for that medicine man," Paul grinned. "Meanwhile, the center continued to flourish, but we soon outgrew the space inside the mobile home."

"Already?" I asked with surprise. "How long had the Bio-Touch Center been in that mobile home?"

"Just about six months. One day I was driving my truck through town when I noticed a 'for lease' sign posted in the window of the vacant Mancos Hotel. I pulled over and stared at the place, imagining how perfect it would be as the center's next location. I was told that the hotel had six bedrooms on the first floor, each with a bathroom. There was also a dining hall, library, meeting room, and a full-sized kitchen. Upstairs were fifteen bedrooms with dormitory style bathrooms."

I let out a low whistle. "It sounds like it was huge."

"Oh, yeah. There was plenty of room to spread out. We needed that space. When I told Cheryl, she loved the idea.

"I needed to know if the practitioners and volunteers were willing to work hard to make the move happen. And sure enough, everyone agreed that the hotel would be perfect. They assured me that they were on board and ready to help."

"So it was a done deal?"

"Not just yet," Paul said, wagging a finger in the air. "I still had the issue of price to deal with. The advertised monthly rent for the hotel was too steep for us, but the place was ideal, so I just couldn't give up. I had several meetings with the owner, explaining to him what the hotel was going to be used for, and how helpful our services were to the whole community. He was a businessman, but a guy with a heart. He finally agreed to lower the rent to what we could afford.

"Then we got busy. We cleaned, scraped, and painted, topping it all off with our newly erected sign. Cheryl and I then moved into the new center. We became the caretakers, making sure everything was ready every morning before the doors opened for the day's activities."

"What was a typical day like?"

"Recipients chatted and snacked as they waited for their sessions, just as they had done before. There were five alternating practitioners giving sessions in the five rooms six days a week. We were completely booked. Through word of mouth, people from all over the country were signing up to take classes and have sessions.

"Our practitioner training class ran two days, but the certification class was ten days in length. So, we hosted four students at a time. They stayed at the center until the conclusion of their class. We charged a modest fee, which included room and board, class materials, and all the training. Every ten days a new group of four students would arrive for classes.

"During that time, a community of people began to develop around the center. Some of them volunteered their cooking and baking skills in the kitchen, while others donated their time helping with laundry, cleaning, and whatever else needed to be done."

"You must have been in heaven. You were back in the community-type setting that you loved, and generating a lot of interest in Bio-Touch."

"Yes," Paul nodded, "It was great. I enjoyed how the new center was a hive of activity. I loved feeling the positive energy as more and more people shared and learned Bio-Touch. We started offering philosophical lectures to students and practitioners one night each week. Grandfather and Norman were our alternating guest speakers. Grandfather would speak on a variety of complex spiritual topics, and Norman spoke on aspects of healing.

"I remember the days I stood in the back of the room, watching the practitioners and students during those lectures. I was so pleased with how things were turning out, I wanted to pinch myself to make sure I wasn't dreaming. Grandfather and Norman were so different from each other in style and personality—yet both were caring and dedicated. I was proud to call them mentors of mine, just as my old friend Guy was. Actually, each of them taught me different important lessons, and Bio-Touch was the ultimate culmination of those teachings," Paul said. "It was the perfect blending of Guy's 'love thy neighbor' principles, of Grandfather's spiritually enlightening concepts, and Norman's knowledge of outer body work. In other words, a unification of all the teachings to that point, consolidating the truth that love, body, and spirit are all intertwined."

"Wow. I love it when things come together so beautifully," I said.

"And," Paul continued, "it reminded me of when Jesus was asked, 'Master, which is the great commandment in the law?' Jesus answered by saying, 'Thou shalt love the Lord thy God with all thy heart, and with all thy soul, and with all thy mind. This is the first and great commandment. And the second is like unto it. Thou shalt love thy neighbor as thyself. On these two commandments hang all the laws and the prophets.' And, Debra, that's what crystallized for me. By practicing Bio-Touch, I learned that God, Neighbor, and Self are a trilogy of one, united in love."

"Absolutely perfect," I said, as goosebumps sprouted on my arms. It felt like one of those moments in life that should be accompanied by the glorious strains of Beethoven's Ninth. "Paul, I'm curious to hear about your recipients at that time. Could you tell me about the people who were actually being healed back then? Any interesting stories there?"

"Oh, yes. There was Curtis. Even though it's been nearly twenty-five years, he's one recipient whose story still amazes me."

I turned to a fresh page of my writing pad, eager to capture what he was about to tell me. "I'm ready," I announced.

"Curtis was getting up in age. He was blind. And Bio-Touch helped him to see."

"Well, I certainly wasn't expecting to hear you say that!" I exclaimed. "You mean like, 'and on that day the eyes of the blind shall see?'"

"Yep, that's usually the reaction I get when I talk about the blind man. I either get a biblical reference or total skepticism," Paul said laughing. "But it's understandable. That kind of story evokes emotion."

"Well, I can't wait to hear it. Lay it on me."

"I could tell it to you, but I have a better idea. Have you ever looked through the book of testimonials we keep at the Bio-Touch Center?" he asked.

"You mean that three-ringed notebook? I've flipped through it a couple of times, but I've never sat down to read the testimonials. Why?"

Paul smiled. "Because Curtis' story is in there, just exactly as he wrote it," he answered softly. "It's fairly long, but I think you'll find it worth reading."

"You don't want to tell me the short version now?"

"No," Paul answered, "I know Curtis will tell it better."

Suddenly I was dying to read that story. I couldn't wait to get my hands on the testimonial notebook, so I stopped at the center the next day to grab it. As I carried it to the car, I felt a sense of awe. Each of the book's contributors had felt compelled to share their story so that others might benefit. Although I had errands to run, I drove right home, hungry to read every word.

I wasn't disappointed. Many of the stories deeply moved me. And even though his were the ones I couldn't wait to devour, I purposely saved Curtis' words for last. I had a feeling they'd make a fine dessert. After all, who could resist a blind man's testimonial? This is what he wrote:

IT HAS TO DO WITH HEALING!

And consequently, improving my mental attitude. It has happened to many people in this regard, and I want to relate the story exactly as it happened without any imagination . . . without any recourse to embellishment or any of that sort of thing. I'll do my best to be straight and honest.

To begin with, I'm a blind man. In our family, we have a blindness that's hereditary. It is called retinitis pigmentosa . . . better known as RP. Half the men go blind every other generation. The female carries the recessive gene for this blindness. They give it to their sons, but they don't get it themselves. They pass it on to their daughters in the form of a recessive gene. Needless to say, I've been blind . . . totally blind . . . for about five or six years.

It's been a slow thing and steadily. In this generation, there are eight of us with this blindness. The next generation I know of has two, but they are very young yet, and probably don't know that they have it. At any rate, I am a blind man.

I also have leukemia . . . CLL. That means chronic lymphocytic leukemia . . . the least oppressive type. I've been told I have about eleven years to live. A lot of that has to do with a person's physical condition and mental attitude.

I used to have a fishing buddy who'd take me fishing, and we got along famously. Some time went by and I talked to him one day and he sounded like I wouldn't be seeing him anymore. He had brittle diabetes. He was a brittle diabetic, I should say, and was in very bad shape. It was only a few months after that (perhaps six months) when I was at a funeral and I saw him and I heard him speaking to me and he sounded just like he did when we went fishing. He sounded like his old self. I asked him, "What in the world has hap-pened to you? You sound wonderful."

He told me he would call me and tell me about it, which in the course of time he did. When he called, he said he'd found out about a process akin to the laying on of hands, but it was a little more detailed than that by a long shot. He said it was called Bio-Touch. He said it was a new process . . . just a matter of a few years back, and it was brought to light, and is now a really going concern. He took me there.

I'm sorry, but I am very much of a skeptic on anything. I'm a skeptic on ways to make money and ways for someone to take it away from you. In spite of this, I am not the type of person to be blunt or rude, and if they had done this for my friend, then perhaps there was something to it. So, I acquiesced to being treated.

First thing I noticed from the treatment was being lightly touched in a very methodic way. It made me feel a little strange. After the treatment the practitioners were very nice and warm. They said there was no charge. They were all volunteers and their main concern was to help people and see them get better. I wondered in my mind if they saw many people getting better. Of course I had to admit . . . there was my friend.

So we left. I experienced some unnatural, but rather gratify-ing results. They had told me that after the treatment, I might feel some old pains or some strange little discomforts here and there that wouldn't amount to anything and would go away soon. I had had a hard blow on the kidneys many years ago, which lasted for a month or so, but suddenly that afternoon I recognized the pain I had had in my kidney those many years ago. It hurt, but only for a minute or so, but the pain was recognized as exactly the pain I had had before.

Still being skeptical, I laid it to my imagination or a coinci-dence. But it was enough to tickle my interest, so I went to the cen-ter again. And I continued to go. The practitioners were always so kind and concerned. Again they said there was no charge, but if I felt so inclined, to put a donation in the pot. That proved to me that there was certainly no scam involved.

I kept going week after week and kept feeling better. My white blood count had been as high as 196,000. It should be 10,000. At that time I had felt like I was going to die, but the doctor put me on a mild chemotherapy which brought it down, and that was before I was going to Bio-Touch. The usual thing was that it continued to go up steadily. And it did a little, and then it came back to 39,000. It went back and forth, and made me wonder. My doctor said, "Well, that's just a peculiarity with yourself." I accepted that.

Then the practitioners were working on my eyes, and never giving up. For a blind man to see again is virtually unheard of, except under the hands of the Almighty. Well, they never gave up and I kept feeling better. Every time I would have a treatment, I would feel wonderful, sometimes two, three days after. My treatments went down to twice a week and I still felt good. My leukemia just didn't bother me at all, even though sometimes the count would go up fairly high and then down again.

Then I began to think . . . goodness I can see the light by the window . . . a glow of light, and I got quite excited. I was convinced Bio-Touch was doing things for me. To see after all that darkness! That light was just so exciting . . . astounding. As time went on, it continued to get a little better. I couldn't really identify anything, for I really couldn't see anything.

When I went outside everything was dark grey, and inside everything was black. But as time went on, I could see that I was outside. I could see a lighter grey. Then things began to appear, and I thought it was just my imagination. It's hard to tell when you are beginning to see something. It's hard to describe it. It's like a collage . . . seen through a thick fog...there would be an odd little pattern.

But then one morning, just a few months ago, I went into the bathroom and turned on the light as I always do. I looked in the mirror, and there I saw the ugliest old man I had ever seen! His eyes were dark sockets. He had white-white hair over him. It shook me up, for I realized it was me that I was actually seeing. I couldn't believe it. I wasn't impressed with what I was looking at, but what excitement! As I looked, I looked harder and harder, and it faded away. And I thought—did I really see that? Yes. I knew I had. I went to Bio-Touch all excited and told them about it, and it was as though they were seeing . . . they were so excited for me.

The last big thing that happened to me was one day when we were riding home from Mancos. I thought I saw a light out of the corner of my eye. I looked over to the right and there was the most beautiful sight I had ever seen—after my wife. Looking over there I saw those two great mountains. I had no idea those mountains were that high. We were coming down into Cherry Creek. In the sky were flimsy clouds. The sun had gone down behind one of the mountains, and it was shining on those clouds. Such a beautiful sunset. I was astounded. I told them what I was seeing. I described it, and they said that was right. I could see what I thought were trees on one mountain and followed it up as high as it would go, but by then it was only a matter of a minute or so and it started fading out. But I had seen!! That scene has been seared into my mind. I take it out periodically to see it. It was beautiful!

Since then, things have kept getting a little plainer. I would see things like the edge of a door. Thinking it was further away than it was, I usually bumped into it. My head is covered with bumps. But that was such a thrill.

And now I can look outside. Prior to seeing that sunset, I had looked out the back window and looked to where a certain tree was. I could see that tree! I used to look at it to see how much sight I was losing . . . that is before everything had gone black. It had slowly over the days disappeared. I looked out there and there was that tree! I could see it and could almost follow it to the top. This had to be in the morning before the sun was up. I looked towards the northeast where the tree was. I could even see spaces between the branches. It was a ponderosa pine tree. Then after seeing the sunset, I started looking out there again . . . and I can see to the top of that tree. It's all very fuzzy. Anything I see is fuzzy, except that sunset and my face in the mirror. The tree stays there for awhile, and then it slowly disappears.

The same thing has been happening to me with my leukemia. My white count would slowly climb up, and I am now on chemotherapy again. It's so mild that it hasn't really bothered me. The white count is coming down now.

What I'm writing this for is the miracle of Bio-Touch. In my mind, I think it's the laying on of hands . . . the original way and the proper way. Christ did such healings and told us we would do greater than this. I keep thinking: is this possibly what he meant? Is it possibly going to heal millions of people—that people can minister one to another with the same candor and unselfishness? It could be . . . it very easily could be.

Curtis T.

Age 74

I closed the book with a deep sigh. I could see why Paul hadn't forgotten Curtis. And now I understood why he wanted me to read the man's words for myself. Curtis's descriptions of being blind were exquisite, helping me to understand, to a small degree, that difficult challenge. To be able to share in Curtis's joy and gratitude at being able to see again, was an honor.

With closed eyes, I leaned back in my chair trying to imagine seeing the world through the streaky grey mist inside my lids. It was incomprehensible. But Curtis was able to escape that darkness, if only for short periods of time. He could drink in the light and see a mountain, a tree, and himself in the mirror. No wonder he called Bio-Touch a miracle.

CHAPTER ELEVEN

Through the Years

Never doubt that a small group of thoughtful, committed citizens
can change the world; indeed, it's the only thing that ever has.

Margaret Mead

"Looks like things were going great guns for Bio-Touch when we left off last week," I said, looking over the pages of my notes. "The center had moved into the Old Mancos Hotel, and people from around the country were showing up for sessions and classes.

"That's correct," Paul nodded, as he took his usual spot on the couch. His trusty green water bottle stayed by his side.

"What year was that, again?" I asked, searching for my timeline.

"That was the summer of 1990. Six months later in January of 1991, my friend Daryl told me he was planning his first trip to Hawaii. He was headed to Oahu, so I told him he should call my brother, Bruce, who lived on the island with his wife and their little girl. My dad and his wife, Hilde, lived on the island too. So, once Daryl got to the island," Paul continued, "he called Bruce. They even met for lunch. At that time, Bruce and I hadn't seen each other in ten years."

"Why hadn't you seen him in so long?"

"As you know, I dropped out of the family for years while I was living on the land. And even after we moved back to civilization, Cheryl and I still practiced the philosophy of erasing personal history, so we avoided contacting our family and friends."

"Oh, you were still doing that?" I asked with a grimace.

"Yes, we were still doing that. So during their lunch, Daryl told Bruce about Bio-Touch, and how I had devoted my life to it. Then Bruce told Daryl that he missed having me in his life, and had been trying to figure out a way to get me to Hawaii for our father's upcoming seventieth birthday celebration. Now he had the perfect way to not only get me there, but maybe entice me to stay in Hawaii, too."

"How could he do that?" I asked.

"By convincing me that Hawaii needed Bio-Touch. Over the next week, Bruce spent his spare time visiting health food stores and spiritual bookstores talking to anyone who'd listen. He explained Bio-Touch to them, gauging their level of interest. He talked to people for hours each day, learning things he'd never heard of before. He took notes on everything they said, studying the information until he felt ready to call me.

"When he dialed the phone number for the Bio-Touch Center, Cheryl answered, identifying herself as Cheryl Bucky. Bruce was shocked. He didn't know I'd re-married."

"That's sad. Erasing personal history sure kills the bond between family members," I said.

"Exactly! So when I got on the phone," Paul continued, "Bruce immediately launched into his prepared text. He asked me if I knew Hawaii was a spiritual place. He said the people there had incredible auras around them, and higher consciousness, minds, and energies. Then he said there were many star children there, who were in touch with their souls."

"What are star children?"

"Apparently, they're souls who've been sent to earth from all over the universe to help the planet, bring peace, raise consciousness, and fix all the corrupt governments. They've been given a special assignment to assist in the earth's rebirth."

"Well that sounds lovely, but if they're really here, they must be sleeping on the job," I said.

"No, they probably have their hands pretty full right now," Paul said. "Anyway, Bruce was convincing. He assured me that the people of Hawaii needed Bio-Touch. Then he said he'd be willing to pay Cheryl's and my way there for a visit. We could stay at his house for as long as we needed to, and all he asked in return, was for us to attend Dad's birthday party.

"Cheryl and I talked it over, intrigued with the idea of bringing Bio-Touch to Hawaii. So I called Bruce the next day to say that Cheryl and I would come to the party. And two weeks later we arrived at his house."

"Weren't you uncomfortable staying in Bruce's home after not seeing him for so long?" I asked.

"Maybe a little bit, at first. After all, I had not attended his and Shari's wedding and had never met my niece, Molly. She only knew me as the uncle who lived in a teepee in the mountains."

"She should have taken you to school for show-and-tell," I said, laughing. "I'm sure none of the other kids had an uncle who bathed with beavers."

"Probably not." Paul chuckled. "Anyway, it didn't take long for me and Cheryl to feel completely at home with them. Bruce and Shari even redecorated the spare bedroom for us. But we were more comfortable sleeping on a futon on their screened-in porch—called a lanai."

"Really? Why was that?" I asked, already knowing the answer.

Paul gestured towards the ceiling. "Because we could see the stars through the roof, breathe in the fresh air, and smell the blossoming trees. We also had a nice view of the mountains. Occasionally, we could even hear the ocean."

"When you describe it like that, it sounds nice," I admitted. "So, how was your dad's party?"

"It was great. My father was happy and surprised to see Cheryl and me among the guests. He actually met her when we lived on the land. And it was nice to see friends and family I hadn't seen in a long time."

"Wait a minute, Paul. I'm confused about something," I said. "Since you and Cheryl were still erasing personal history, why was it okay for you to visit family and attend your dad's party? What am I missing here?"

"Good question. You see, Cheryl and I stopped practicing erasing personal history when I decided to totally embrace Bio-Touch. That day at Grandfather's house, after I received the letter from Kevin's mother, was the day everything changed. I knew once I went down the path to Bio-Touch, I'd have to put my personal path aside. That time of my life was over. Now it was time for me to be of service to others. Bio-Touch was the reason I stepped back into the real world. And that's why it was time to embrace my family and friends again."

"Speaking of embracing family, where was your mother living?"

"She lived in Denver."

I nibbled the end of my pen. "Had you welcomed her back into your life yet?"

"No, I hadn't," Paul said with a wry smile, "and I'm sure you're chomping at the bit to hear how that went down. But I'll save that story for our next meeting, if you don't mind."

I shrugged my shoulders. "Why should I mind?"

Paul rolled his eyes. "Meanwhile, back in Honolulu, Cheryl and I spent days walking the streets, talking to people, and getting a feel for their receptiveness to Bio-Touch. Everything Bruce said was true. People seemed excited about it.

"Then Bruce surprised us with a generous gift. Months before, he signed a contract with a local radio station for five commercials a day, five times a week, to endorse his leasing company. A monthly one-hour talk show was included in that contract. Unfortunately, he didn't receive a single call after more than one hundred commercials and five talk shows. He realized he could use his contract to help spread the word about Bio-Touch, so he gave his remaining live radio shows to Cheryl and me. He wished us better luck than he'd had.

"Cheryl and I were grateful to him, and excited to be interviewed by the show's host on a live radio show. But the woman acted cold, not even trying to hide her cynicism as she asked us questions. Eventually she thawed, though, becoming more interested in our answers. Toward the end of the hour, we announced that we were offering a training class to be held later that week. The switchboard immediately lit up with callers asking questions and wanting to sign up. There were so many interested people, we divided the class into two. We taught fifty students over the next two weekends."

"Wow, that's a lot. And did those students convince you to stay?" I asked.

"Actually, on the last day of class one of the students, an elderly Chinese gentleman, had tears in his eyes telling me how much Hawaii needed Bio-Touch—how much Hawaii needed me. And deep-down, I knew he was right. Although Bruce said the same thing, hearing it from that man really illuminated it for me.

"After spending three productive weeks in Hawaii, Cheryl and I returned to Mancos. We couldn't wait to share everything with Norman and Carole, so we went right to their house. The prospect of setting up a Bio-Touch Center in Honolulu seemed like a reality to us already. But we wanted to hear what they had to say and, hopefully, receive their blessing."

"And did you receive it?" I asked.

"Yes. Norman actually encouraged us to go ahead and set up the sister center there. He said he and Carole would keep the Mancos Center going. So two months later, in April of 1991, Cheryl and I relocated to Honolulu, taking all our clothes and possessions in just a few suitcases."

"Everything you owned fit into a few bags?"

"Of course. You haven't forgotten how we simplified our lives, have you?"

"No, how could I forget that?" I cringed picturing the over-stuffed suitcases—two large, two medium, and two garment bags—that Howard and I dragged along on a recent fifteen night cruise.

"So," Paul continued, "we lived on Bruce and Shari's lanai for awhile. We were busy looking at inexpensive rental properties to house the Bio-Touch Center. We found a place that was small, but pleasant. It didn't need a lot of work, so the doors of the new center opened in a matter of weeks.

"However," he said, his eyebrows rising, "it was located on the second floor of a building that didn't have an elevator. So, the only way to reach it was by trudging up forty cement steps. People arrived huffing and puffing, saying it was like making a pilgrimage to Mecca. Of course we hadn't planned it that way, but the similarity to trekking up to Norman and Carole's house made it seem perfect.

"Things progressed quickly. It didn't take long before we were incorporated as a non-profit in the state of Hawaii. Word was spreading about us, so more and more people showed up for sessions and classes. In fact, the center became so busy, we asked Joyzelle, a friend and certified practitioner from Mancos, if she could make Honolulu her temporary home. Lucky for us, she was able to fly out immediately, helping that center get off to a smooth start."

"Was it just word of mouth that was causing so much interest in Bio-Touch?" I asked.

"Mostly, but occasionally we went back on the air to inform more people about the sessions and classes. Then we began writing newsletters that highlighted the center's activities. We listed the names of our new graduate and certified practitioners, and schedules of upcoming classes. Soon we added testimonials from recipients, as well. The newsletters were mailed quarterly to all practitioners and recipients."

"I had fun reading through those old newsletters you kept," I said. "They were informative and well-written. So, with things going so well in Hawaii, why did you open a Bio-Touch Center in Arizona?"

Paul sipped some water before answering. "In late 1992 a married couple I knew, who took certified practitioner classes in Colorado, decided that their hometown of Lake Havasu City, Arizona needed a Bio-Touch Center. They contacted me wanting to meet and discuss the possibility. Then Cheryl and I made several trips to Arizona over a span of months to visit the area, and talk to locals."

"Those trips must have been expensive—even in those days. How could you afford the airfare?"

"Our organization had the money to cover those kinds of costs. It's been in the black since its inception. There were funds available for the day-to-day operations, as well as for future expansion. But to cover my personal expenses, I washed cars."

"You worked at a carwash?" I asked.

"No, I was hired by a man who owned a mobile car-washing business," Paul explained. "I was part of a crew of four guys who drove a truck to car dealerships all over Oahu and washed hundreds of cars on the lots. The truck had a mounted water tank and soap dispenser along with a pressure washer. I earned a percentage on each washed car. It paid the bills; I did it for years. Cheryl and I did all sorts of odd jobs, including housecleaning, to make ends meet.

"Meanwhile after visiting and studying the area, Cheryl and I agreed that a Bio-Touch Center in Lake Havasu City would be a good idea. We did everything necessary to lay the groundwork for the Center's opening—including teaching classes. At first the center was run inside that couple's home. But then they rented space in an office building. We applied, and became incorporated in Arizona as a non-profit. And things went well . . . for a while."

"Uh oh. What happened?"

Paul's forehead furrowed. "After only eight months, the couple began to question how and why things had to be done a certain way.

They wanted to change things. They even wanted to add their own points to the manual. Cheryl and I spent lots of time on the phone with them patiently explaining why they had to stay within our guidelines."

"Were you able to convince them?"

"Not at all," Paul replied. "But we didn't have to. Our foundation was formed to ensure and maintain the integrity of Bio-Touch for all practitioners sharing the technique around the globe. The organization created strong guidelines to be followed, while still walking the fine line between strict limitations—which served to protect the basic principles—and freedom to consider new ideas.

"That's why we were determined to protect the purity of Bio-Touch, and committed to making sure that everyone learned the points exactly as shown in the manual," he emphasized. "It was as important then as it is now. As Bio-Touch passes from generation to generation, we must keep it the same, simple technique that anyone can practice."

I rested my chin in the palm of my hand. "So, how'd you resolve the issue?"

"It resolved itself after we pulled all our support," Paul answered. "The couple insisted that they were going to continue running the center their own way. So, I told them they could run it anyway they wanted, and call it anything they wanted except Bio-Touch. They knew, legally, they had no choice but to comply."

"So, what happened then?"

"They decided to close the center, after all. One day we received a letter at the center in Hawaii informing us of their decision. I remember how Cheryl and I sat with Joyzelle on a Friday afternoon, having a beer and talking about what to do. We didn't want to give up the Arizona corporate structure since it took a lot of time and money to set up. So, we decided to open a Center in a different city in Arizona."

"And how'd you decide on Tucson?"

"Joyzelle and I had been there before, and really liked the culture and the rustic feel. Within weeks, Joyzelle moved to Tucson with a friend, another woman who was a practitioner in Hawaii. They just packed up and moved, finding a tiny apartment to rent by the University of Arizona.

"They held classes and gave sessions in that apartment. Cheryl and I flew in from Hawaii to help them. We gave workshops, put announcements in the local papers, and I gave interviews on two radio shows. By the fall of 1993, interest in Bio-Touch was slowly but surely spreading in Tucson.

"In less than a year, we moved the Bio-Touch Center to office space on 5th Street. It was a small center—just two session rooms with a waiting area. Oh, and get ready for this—there was no bathroom. The bathroom was actually located outside, past the courtyard. In order to wash our hands before giving sessions, we installed a sink close to the desk in the waiting room. But there were no water pipes to hook the sink up to, so we hauled water from outside in a big container with a spigot. After washing our hands, the water drained into a bucket underneath the sink."

"Ugh. How antiquated. You must have loved it."

Paul smiled. "It worked fine. You'd have hated it. A few years later, a group of us constructed a third room, and fixed up the waiting area."

"That's nice. But you didn't add a bathroom? Or even a sink with running water?"

"We couldn't. There weren't any water lines leading to the offices," he said. "One day a collection agency bought the building. We stayed. Then the local Republican Headquarters moved in. We still stayed. I'm sure we were considered the weird ones in that building."

"Probably so," I said with a laugh. "So at that point it was 1994. What was happening with the Hawaiian Bio-Touch Center? How were you keeping both Centers going? Were you and Cheryl still traveling back and forth?"

"Yeah, we were racking up plenty of frequent flyer miles. Luckily, we had the help of quite a few volunteers who were giving sessions and classes at both centers, as well as establishing our outreach programs."

"What was the purpose of the outreach programs?" I asked.

"They were a good way to spread the word about Bio-Touch—by reaching out to the community, giving presentations to civic groups, medical centers, community colleges, and places like that," he explained. "One of our certified practitioners, John, even gave a presentation at the Halawa Prison in Honolulu. Bio-Touch was so well received by the inmates there, John was invited back on a regular basis to teach more and more inmates how to share it with others. A local

Hawaiian community organizer said that Bio-Touch was the first thing the inmates had ever learned that they could call their own. It was a tool that no one could ever take away from them. She said that Bio-Touch was the kind of positive glue that could hold communities together.

"And with all that going on," Paul continued, "somehow we still found time to travel to other islands and to cities on the mainland, giving workshops."

"Whew. You never did anything half-way, did you?"

Paul's face lit up. "No way. I was too exhilarated by all the interest in Bio-Touch. We all thrived on the opportunities to reach out and help more people. We were excited to 'just touch' as many folks as possible.

"As a matter of fact," he added, "by 1996 the center in Hawaii had given over four thousand sessions, racking up over six thousand volunteer hours, while the center in Tucson had given almost six thousand sessions totaling seventy-five hundred volunteer hours."

"Very impressive, Paul. That was a lot of touching in a few years. So, what else was going on that led to Bio-Touch's growth?"

"Well in Tucson, we were featured in the local newspaper, on a public access television channel, and on a local television news program during one of their health segments. We received over a hundred calls at the center in the twenty-four hour period following that show.

"And then we produced a training video, knowing it would be an important supplement to the manual. We wanted it to be professional, but we couldn't spend a lot of money. That goal was accomplished with the help of two of our certified practitioners, Kim and Rachel. They graciously donated the camera crew, cameras, and use of the studio in Honolulu. Besides producing, they also were the directors. Taping was done over three days and nights. Practitioners were filmed touching the correct points on their recipient's bodies. I assumed the role of host, narrating, introducing, and concluding the video. When it was finished, Kim and Rachel spent hours editing."

"And how did you feel about the results?" I asked.

"We were thrilled," Paul answered. "It was perfect. Beautiful Hawaiian sights and sounds were transitioned between the sets of points, the introduction, and the conclusion. And the music was specially created for us, too."

"Well, I can certainly attest to how well-done that video was," I said. "Of course I had the DVD version, but I must have watched it forty times while I was interning and trying to learn all the points. I'm a visual learner, so it was extremely helpful for me."

"Yeah, most people find it worthwhile.

"Meanwhile back in Colorado, the Mancos Center eventually closed. Norman retired to a small town in Arizona where he died in 2003. But Cheryl kept in touch with Carole—they're still friends, in fact," Paul answered. "That's another great thing about Bio-Touch. It's a method instead of being based on the leaderships of one person, so its effectiveness is never dependent on human changes, issues, or problems. It doesn't matter because Bio-Touch will still be pristine and unsoiled. It never hinges on the dramas surrounding people."

"While we're on the subject of your mentors, whatever happened to Grandfather?" I asked.

"Grandfather continued to live in that mobile home we bought for him in Mancos until he died in 1994. Cheryl and I went back there to visit him a number of times before he passed away."

"So that's how you knew about the strokes and gangrene Grandfather had at the end of his life," I said. "And your first mentor, Guy? Whatever happened to him?"

"Guy died back in 1988, before I even met Norman. Cheryl and I were living in Mancos and working at the grocery store when he died."

"He was fairly young, wasn't he?" I asked.

"Yes, but hard living and a lot of beer can kill you early. I'd say he was in his mid-sixties. I remember thinking—after they all died—how it was my job, now, to really grow up and pass on all the teachings that I'd gotten from them."

"Grow up? You were over fifty when Norman died, Peter Pan."

Paul nodded, chuckling. "You know age is just a number, right?"

"Sure. I keep telling myself that with each passing birthday," I sighed. "So, what other special things were happening for Bio-Touch at that time?"

"Well, by 2000, our community outreach had continued to find opportunities to share Bio-Touch all over Hawaii and Tucson. We gave mini sessions to people at hospitals, baby fairs, senior centers, health fairs, cystic fibrosis walks, heart association walks, and even at the Salvation Army.

"We were giving Bio-Touch sessions every week at a residential teaching and therapeutic community called Amity, located just outside Tucson's city limits. Residents of Amity came from all over the country for a chance to change their lives—to become free of substance abuse, and take responsibility for their actions."

"And how was Bio-Touch able to benefit them?" I asked.

"Well, the sessions certainly eased their aches and pains. But their stress levels came down significantly, which seemed to be of key importance in helping them stay drug-free.

"Also, I met Dr. Gary Schwartz, who was director of the Human Energy Systems Laboratory at the University of Arizona. He agreed to work with me on a research project to see if scientific methods could define the effectiveness of Bio-Touch. But before the experiments began, Gary said to me, 'What if the experiments prove Bio-Touch isn't effective?'"

"How did you answer him? And why did you encourage those research experiments in the first place?"

"Because many people asked me over the years why there wasn't any research on Bio-Touch. I knew they would welcome such validation," Paul answered. "And frankly, even after all the amazing things I'd seen with Bio-Touch, there was still one part of my mind that sought 'proof' that it really worked. But in answering Gary's question, I told him that if Bio-Touch was proven to be ineffective, I'd just retire and go back to living in the mountains."

"And what'd he say to that?"

"He loved my answer," Paul grinned. "He said most people would insist that the object of their life's focus was effective, no matter what the research showed. The first experiment included a survey given to about six hundred recipients at the centers in Hawaii and Tucson and at the Amity facility. Surveys were also given to recipients at a center we had at the time in Yuba City, California. We ran that center for a few years, but it never blossomed in that location. Anyway, all those recipients filled out forms before and after their Bio-Touch sessions. The after-session forms asked whether or not they felt less stress, less pain, more relaxed, and more energetic."

"And what were the results?" I asked.

"Overwhelmingly, recipients reported decreases in stress and pain and increases in energy and feelings of relaxation following a session. Another experiment added blood pressure and heart rate readings recorded before and midway through recipient's sessions. Again, the subjects reported decreases in their stress and pain, and increases in relaxation and also feelings of being cared for, as evidenced by the results on the blood pressure and heart rate monitors."

"Those sound like significant findings," I said.

"Yes, they were. And even though the results didn't really surprise me, I was grateful to Gary for providing the opportunity for all the parts of my mind to finally be satisfied," Paul said.

"There were other studies done as well, weren't there?"

"Yes. Around that same time, Dr. Kenna Stephenson, a family physician, became familiar with Bio-Touch when she worked as the associate medical director at St. Elizabeth of Hungary Clinic in Tucson. The clinic provided medical and dental care for people without health insurance. One of our practitioners, Sister Mary, visited the clinic a few times a week, giving Bio-Touch sessions to the patients.

"One day," Paul continued, "Dr. Stephenson, was busy with a full patient schedule, but had a bad headache. The over-the-counter medicine she took didn't touch her pain. When Sister Mary offered to give her a quick Bio-Touch session, she agreed. Her headache disappeared seconds after the session began. Dr. Stephenson was so intrigued that she decided to conduct her own research project.

"She studied eighteen healthy women, ages sixty-two to eighty-four. Half of the women received twenty minute Bio-Touch sessions once a week for four weeks. The other half did not receive Bio-Touch, agreeing to abstain from any touch interaction including massages, other touch therapies, and even manicures or pedicures for the duration of the study.

"Using blood and saliva analysis, their levels of blood-clotting factors, inflammatory factors, cortisol, estradiol, progesterone, testosterone, and immune factors were measured at the beginning of the study, as well as every other week.

"After the four weeks, the half who received Bio-Touch showed a significant increase in interleukin-12, an immune system molecule known to increase resistance to infection and cancer. They also exhibited a decrease in levels of cortisol, a hormone from the adrenal glands that reacts to stress.

"And sometime after the study, Dr. Stephenson wrote a book called *Awakening Athena–Resilience, Restoration, and Rejuvenation for Women.* In her book she included the results of that study and devoted a portion of Chapter 7 to the merits of Bio-Touch."

"Wow. There couldn't possibly have been anything else happening at that time, could there?" I asked, scribbling frantically.

"Oh yes there could," Paul beamed. "We had students from far and wide coming for classes at both the Hawaii and Tucson Centers, taking their new-found knowledge back home to cities in California, New Jersey, South Carolina, Texas, Pennsylvania, and other states. And more and more students were coming from other countries as well, taking classes, and then going home to share Bio-Touch in India, England, Germany, Denmark, and the Philippines. The Bio-Touch manual was translated into a number of different languages, including Spanish, German, Japanese, Russian, and Portuguese."

"Hey, that sounds like the start of your dream to share Bio-Touch around the world," I said.

"Exactly. One particular student, Shahrzad, became a certified practitioner while living in Hawaii, and then felt the pull to return to her country of Egypt to share Bio-Touch there," Paul said. "She began giving sessions in her family home, located at the base of the pyramids in Giza. Soon, she had students traveling from as far away as Saudi Arabia and Switzerland for training.

"Then Shahrzad got the opportunity to talk about Bio-Touch on a television show that was broadcast to several Middle Eastern countries. After that show aired, I received emails from people in Egypt, Saudi Arabia, and Lebanon requesting more information. Some of those emails were from medical doctors curious to learn more. It was unbelievable how excited people all over the world were to learn about the power of touch.

"In the summer of 2002, I received a phone call from Shahrzad wondering if I'd consider traveling to Egypt to help her open a Bio-Touch Center there."

"What went through your mind when she asked that?"

"First I wondered if I heard her correctly," Paul said. "Opening a center in the Middle East? My imagination ran wild with images of Bio-Touch bringing peace to people all over the world, and bridging historical differences, healing families, friends, communities, and even our planet.

"But in the meantime," he continued, "the Tucson Center was bursting at the seams in that space we were in for eight years. Cheryl found a new building for us to rent. The place was nice, but it needed work. With the help of a few builders, and an array of volunteers, we widened the bathroom, framed the walls, added lighting, created storage, built cabinets, fixed plumbing issues, painted, and laid carpeting."

"And because of all that work, we have our beautiful Center today. And it even has a bathroom, two sinks, and running water! Great job," I said. "So, did you ever get to Egypt?"

"Yes, I did. In early March of 2003 I flew to Egypt."

"But weren't you scared? You were not only American, but Jewish as well," I stressed, "and the Iraq War was about to start."

"Yeah, that was a bit nerve wracking, but I had to have faith. I had to believe that the opportunity outweighed any risks. It turned out to be amazing. I loved watching Shahrzad teach workshops to students and give sessions to her recipients using the gift I'd brought—a new massage table. By the way, I felt safe and welcome wherever I went in her village. Everyone there knew about her healing work.

"She invited me to accompany her on her second appearance on the Arabic satellite television program. The hour-long show reminded me of *Regis and Kelly Live*. The hosts spoke both Arabic and English and went out of their way to make me feel comfortable. On-air callers clogged the phone lines as I gave a session to one of the show's hosts on the air. Then the crewmembers lined up to be worked on. They suffered with various aches and pains due to the heavy equipment they had to maneuver.

"And as I listened to the translation of what the callers were asking, I realized that they were experiencing the same pains, stresses, and fears that anyone, anywhere, experiences. The human condition was the same for all people, no matter where they lived. And I was absolutely thrilled when the hosts closed the program by saying, 'The message tonight is that we should all just touch each other with love.'"

"That's incredible. So, what was the outcome of your visit?" I asked.

"Well, the Bio-Touch website received hundreds of hits. There were orders for the manual from Lebanon, Syria, Kuwait, Bahrain, and, of course, Egypt. And exactly one week after I returned to Tucson, the Iraq War did break out. Even so, Shahrzad and her practitioners continued to give sessions and classes, having translated the manual into Arabic."

"That must have been so gratifying," I said, dropping my pen to rub my overworked fingers.

"It was truly a highlight—one that I'll never forget."

"Now we're up to 2004," I said, checking my notes. "Did anything interesting happen then?"

"Unfortunately, that was the year our Hawaiian center closed."

"But that center had been open for fourteen years. What happened?"

"Lani, the wonderful woman who ran that office for years, passed away suddenly. There was no one who could commit to running the day-to-day operations once she was gone."

"But where did everyone go?" I asked, shrugging my shoulders. "Where was that busy center you created?"

"There'd been less and less activity there for a while. Classes were no longer being taught. There were fewer and fewer practitioners and recipients."

"Why?" I persisted.

"Cheryl and I had moved to Tucson, along with a number of other energetic people from that center. Even though we frequently flew back to Hawaii, we were mainly concentrating our efforts on the Tucson center. Consequently, all the energy that had given life to the Hawaiian center slowly drained away.

"It was bittersweet," he acknowledged. "It was hard to close that center, but we only needed one center to focus on. That was the Tucson one, which was thriving. A year later in 2005, Dr. Carole McKenzie, a PhD, registered nurse, and certified midwife, took Bio-Touch classes.

She was familiar with alternative healing methods because her daughter was hit by a car years before when she was twelve. The doctors said her daughter would probably be in a vegetative state, and never walk again. But Carole arranged alternative therapies for her daughter in conjunction with the mainstream medical protocols. Her daughter's condition improved so much, she could live a normal life, eventually running marathons and earning a master's degree.

"After taking our classes, Carole was impressed with Bio-Touch. In 2006, when she became Chair of the Division of Nursing at Northwestern Oklahoma State University, she introduced a Bio-Touch training course to the curriculum, giving extra credit to student nurses who learned the technique.

"A year later," Paul continued, "she was instrumental in having Bio-Touch become a required course for her nursing students, as well as for the fourteen faculty members within the nursing program. The school became the only university in the United States with that requirement. In 2007 I began traveling there every August to spend a week teaching juniors the basic Bio-Touch practitioner training, and teaching seniors the graduate practitioner training."

"That must have been rewarding," I said.

"It was great. I loved teaching those young people. They were eager to learn, although many were skeptical at first. Then in 2011 those nursing students participated in a Bio-Touch research project, which included more than two-hundred participants ranging in age from eighteen to seventy-three years. Each was asked to fill out a simple questionnaire, and to list one area of specific pain they had at that time. Before and after their Bio-Touch sessions, they were asked to answer questions regarding their feelings of restlessness, stress, pain, relaxation, and of feeling cared for.

"The results showed a marked decrease in the levels of pain, restlessness, and stress, and a significant increase in participants feeling cared for and relaxed after their Bio-Touch sessions. It was interesting to see how those results replicated the earlier results by Dr. Gary Schwartz and Dr. Kenna Stephenson's projects."

"Absolutely," I said. "More validation proving the effectiveness of Bio-Touch. So, that takes us to the present. What's happening with Bio-Touch now?"

"Well, we started offering continuing education units for massage therapists who take our classes. After completing the practitioner training, they'll receive ten units approved by the National Certification Board for Therapeutic Massage and Bodywork.

"I'm also excited about a program called Integrative Touch for Kids (ITK). It's a non-profit organization dedicated to enhancing the well-being of families of children with special medical needs. It provides them with access to a range of therapeutic services that address mind, body, and spirit to improve awareness and quality of life.

"As you know, our logo is a butterfly representing how light the touching is during a healing session. The butterfly happens to be their symbol, too. For them it represents change and transformation that families experience when they go through the healing retreat programs. And like us, volunteers provide services to the families.

"And as you also know, for the past few summers Bio-Touch practitioners participated in ITK's week-long healing retreat in Tucson. We gave Bio-Touch sessions to special needs children, their siblings, and their parents. We taught them key sets of points so the parents and siblings would know how to work on the special needs children, and each other, when they're at home. It's so gratifying to see how Bio-Touch can enhance the lives of these families. We intend to work with this ITK program for many summers to come.

"Also, I was invited to participate in the second annual Science Spirit and Health Symposium called *Understanding the Science of Energy Medicine.* There were many distinguished speakers including Dr. William Tiller, Dr. Melinda Conner, Dr. Bruce Lipton, and Dr. Gary Schwartz, who did the original research on Bio-Touch.

"When I spoke, I presented Gary's research data, talked about the history of Bio-Touch, and then taught all two hundred and fifty people in the audience how to do some of the points on their seat mates. They touched each other right there. Everyone was laughing. It was a blast. Afterwards, forty people signed up to take our classes."

"That must have been incredible, Paul."

"It always is. It's what I call the 'wow' factor . . . that moment when people know a change is happening in the deepest seat of their consciousness, usually within the first five minutes of a Bio-Touch session."

"Is there always such an effect?"

"Yes, there is always the wow factor. Even if people aren't aware of the change, it just happens."

"Well, to wrap things up for today, I'll ask you one last question. What interesting things are on the horizon for Bio-Touch?"

Paul talked as we walked to the door. "The Arizona Center for Integrative Medicine, here at Tucson's University of Arizona College of Medicine, is starting a program where medical students can take elective courses to learn different types of complementary healing techniques. Bio-Touch is one of those techniques," he answered. "I'll be teaching Bio-Touch to those students who choose to learn it. The program may even expand to having the students 'shadow' some of our practitioners—following them as they give sessions. It'll be great to show those medical students how Bio-Touch can be beneficial as a complementary resource for their patients."

Later, after I cleaned the dinner dishes, I sat out on our patio, thinking of the thousands of people helped by Bio-Touch over the years because of Paul's tireless efforts. Of course, he couldn't have done it without Cheryl, and a veritable army of enthusiastic volunteers. Those caring people gave countless hours of their energy and spirit. Over time, volunteers relocated, retired, passed away, or simply moved on. Thankfully, others came to take their place.

However, the most important thing was how the pure essence of Bio-Touch hadn't changed, one iota, in all that time. Paul had worked tirelessly to guarantee that outcome, even as others tried to modify the healing method. His vigilance in his role as caretaker protected Bio-Touch, keeping it the same simple, effective technique he first embraced long ago in a small Colorado town.

CHAPTER TWELVE

A Most Heartfelt Healing

Mothers and their children are in a category all their own.
There's no bond so strong in the entire world.
No love so instantaneous and forgiving.

—Gail Tsukiyama
Dreaming Water

"Paul," I said, flopping down on the couch, "last week we barely touched on the subject of your mom, remember? Today I'd like to hear all about her."

He smiled. He was at my house for our last formal interview session. "Okay. I'm happy to tell you my mother's story. I think it's the most dramatic Bio-Touch story of all."

"Good. I'm ready." I gripped my pen, pressing it onto the paper. Every hair on my head quivered.

"Back in the fall of 1991, if you remember," Paul said after a deep breath, "Cheryl and I moved to Hawaii. We were staying at Bruce and Shari's house. Joyzelle had joined us, and the three of us were working hard to get the new Bio-Touch Center up and running. Well, one night we were all eating dinner in Bruce and Shari's dining room, talking and laughing, when the phone rang. Bruce answered. He listened a minute, then his face turn serious."

"Why? Who was it?" I asked.

"A nurse at a hospital in Denver said that Vivian, our mother, had been admitted after passing out at work. By the time the paramedics got to her, she was already conscious. But her worried employees thought it best to have her rushed to the hospital. Her heart rate was fluctuating dangerously, so the doctors immediately operated, putting in a temporary pacemaker. The nurse finished by saying she'd keep Bruce posted, but for now, Mom was in the recovery room in stable condition. It sounded like things were under control, but we waited by the phone for any more news."

"How old was your mom?" I asked. "Was she sick or being treated for a medical condition?"

"Mom was in her late sixties, and completely healthy. She wasn't on any medications at all. As we waited, we discussed possible scenarios. It would have been too hard for Bruce or Shari to fly to Denver, because Bruce ran his leasing business himself, and Molly was too young to be without her mother for any length of time. So we decided, if need be, I'd fly to Denver. Cheryl would stay in Hawaii, and run the Bio-Touch Center with Joyzelle.

"Just then the nurse called back, saying Mom's blood pressure had 'bottomed out' and doctors had no idea why. She was being rushed into the operating room for open-heart surgery. I jumped up to pack and was on a plane to Denver the next morning.

"When I finally got to the hospital, they told me my mother had been moved to the Intensive Care Unit. I rushed to that floor, where a nurse said that Mom was in a coma following last night's surgery. She suggested that I make myself comfortable in the waiting area until the doctor came to explain my mother's condition.

"That waiting room was a sad place," Paul said, shaking his head. "People sat on hard chairs, looking scared and worried about their loved ones. Some cried, and some paced, while others just sat staring at soap operas on the television screen. They were desperate, depending on the medical system to tell them what would happen next. I knew they felt the same way I did—powerless and helpless. We had no control over what was happening to our loved ones. All we could do was sit there and wait.

"And while I waited, I thought of how my mother and I hadn't communicated since before I moved onto the land. I'm sure you remember that my dad visited me several times, but Mom never did."

"Yes I remember. And who could blame her?" I said as gently as I could manage. "Your mom was shut out of your life for nearly ten years."

"I didn't shut her out. I made it clear that she was welcome to visit me on the land, anytime."

I became irritated. "Paul, your mother couldn't exchange letters with you, or hear your voice over the phone to assess how you were doing. She couldn't invite you over for dinner, or enjoy your presence at a family picnic. Since her only choices were to either show up on your land, and hope she wasn't interfering in your spiritual growth, or not see you at all, she chose the latter. Good for her. Look, I'm a mom so I can only guess how frustrating and heartbreaking that must have been for her. I'm putting myself in her shoes, and I just want to reach through time and give her a hug."

"Okay, maybe I can explain it this way," Paul said in a patient tone. "In our studies, we learned that personal freedom was vital. Of course I was sad that my mother was hurt. I loved her; I didn't feel good about that. She couldn't understand how I needed to break free of the boxes that society and family dynamics crammed people into. The typical message was that good boys and girls who obeyed received the love they deserved. But if they were bad or defiant, they didn't deserve love. That kind of thing. You see, we're forever trying to please mommy and daddy so they'll love us. Our roles as daughters and sons, mothers and fathers are like a complex dance routine. We try to live up to whatever image our parents have for us, to live up to what's acceptable to them, whether it's right for us or not. Most people never escape that trap. They keep up the pretenses of their roles even though they know, deep inside, they're not being true to themselves. They are not free."

My pen raced across the page capturing Paul's words, but my heart was saying, "He's wrong." I quickly examined my own roles—as daughter, sister, wife, and mother—to see how they measured up to his negative descriptions. I never thought of my loving family ties as serious infringements on my freedom. Or theirs. But should I have? Nah. Those issues never came up, so why would I want to start mucking through minefields looking for problems now? I snapped out of my reverie to see Paul studying me.

"You were deep in thought," he said with a smile.

"Oh, I was just trying to grasp your definition of freedom," I said. "I'm having some trouble with it, but let's get back to your story for now."

Paul nodded. "Okay, so I was in the hospital's waiting room worried about my mom. At that point in her life she was a widow, having lost her husband, Bob, to a heart attack. Bob had been her high school sweetheart, but they re-discovered each other years after their first marriages ended. Mom and Bob were the proverbial 'love birds' who were always together. Mom even helped Bob run his small chemical company, working beside him in the office every day. After his death, she managed the day-to-day operations of the company, with the help of her employees.

"Then Mom's doctor finally came over and sat in the chair next to me. He said that her heart had been accidentally punctured during the insertion of the temporary pacemaker, which was a very rare occurrence. The surgeons had to crack her chest to get that pacemaker out, and then performed a double bypass procedure. Apparently, her arteries were in a state of collapse, and brittle as eggshells. While they were working on her, it was impossible to get enough oxygen to her brain, so she died on the operating table. They managed to bring her back to life, but didn't expect her to live long. He said that if she did live, though, she would probably be in a persistent vegetative state. Then he said he was sorry."

"Good Lord. What went through your mind hearing all that?" I asked.

Paul squared his shoulders. "I was angry and shocked at how Mom's life had been altered in the blink of an eye. One day she was healthy; the next she was an invalid. During my long flight from Hawaii, I mentally prepared myself to handle whatever situation I might find when I arrived. I had purposely avoided institutions, corporations, insurance companies, and other big businesses like our medical system, for many years. But after listening to that doctor, I knew I had no choice but to deal with that damned medical system, because it just screwed up my mother's life, leaving her worse than dead."

"What a nightmare, and so scary to think it could happen to anybody," I said, shaking my head.

"And it was obvious that the doctor and his colleagues had already given up on my mother. So I vowed that I would start giving her Bio-Touch sessions right away, and nobody was going to stop me. A nurse led me to Mom's room. She was hooked up to machines that monitored her bodily functions with beeping noises and blinking lights. Tubes came out of her everywhere. I bent over the bedrail to begin a session, carefully working around her bandages and medical equipment. Immediately, she sighed. It was a subtle sigh, but I knew she felt my touch. I was amazed and grateful, considering the extreme condition she was in.

"I was told that Mom was in a coma, and that she wouldn't know I was there, or be able to hear or communicate with me at all. But I knew I made a connection with her. Her tiny sigh proved to me that nothing quite connects people like human touch. Nothing reassures us that we're not alone on this planet, more than being touched by another person. So, I whispered in her ear, 'I'm right here with you, Mom, and I know you know that.' And right then and there, I made the commitment to give her Bio-Touch sessions every six hours around the clock to help her get through her ordeal."

"What did you do between sessions?" I asked.

"I took care of practical matters. I called Bruce and Cheryl, filling them in on the latest developments. I also visited with Mom's employees at the chemical company, doing what I could to help out around her office. I slept at Mom's house, taking care of maintenance needs there.

"A few days later, while I was giving my supposedly 'comatose and unaware' mother a session, she suddenly turned to a nurse in the room and said, 'This is my son, Paul.'"

"No way! She said it that casually?"

"Yes. I couldn't believe it," Paul answered. "And you should have seen that nurse's shocked face. It was priceless. There were several more times Mom was able to speak, but only during Bio-Touch sessions. Whenever I witnessed those moments of Mom's lucidity, I knew she was still there inside her broken body. I knew that Bio-Touch was the spark keeping me 'in touch' with her.

"There were other incredible things happening, too. Not being a medically trained person, though, I didn't realize their significance until the nurses told me. For instance, Mom required very few medications. Even though she just endured two heart surgeries, and was lying immobile in bed, she needed only a small dose of diuretics to keep her fluids moving. And she needed no heart or pain medications whatsoever, which was unheard of. Patients in her dire condition usually needed large doses of both.

"Several times, Mom's blood pressure fluctuated dangerously, and the warning alarms on the monitors went crazy. A medical team rushed in, wanting to administer drugs. But I asked them to wait a minute while I began a session on her. I knew my touch would help right away, so I didn't mind the glares I got from the team impatiently waiting for me to finish.

"And you know what? Those monitors went back to normal right in front of their eyes as I touched my mother!" Paul exclaimed. "That happened with her blood pressure, heart rate, and oxygen saturation levels as well. The medical staff was astonished whenever that happened. They never got used to watching me touch Mom for a minute, and then not having to give her medications after all."

"But what did they think you were doing, Paul? Did they ask you?"

"They did. And when I explained, most of them were fascinated. They saw how Mom's condition stabilized during sessions. But some were annoyed with me, barely tolerating my presence. Once I overheard a couple of nurses gossiping about me. They said they weren't sure what to make of me; I wasn't like anyone they'd ever met before."

I placed my forefinger on my chin. "Gee, I can't imagine why they thought that."

"They even referred to me as 'that hippie in a Hawaiian shirt.'"

I burst out laughing. "Well, how did you know they meant you? Maybe there were other long-haired, bearded, sandal-wearing guys in palm tree outfits placing their fingers on patients."

"No, I'm pretty sure I was the only one," Paul said with a chuckle. "I developed a good rapport with a few of those nurses and staff people, though. They went above and beyond when they cared for my mother. And they answered my endless questions with patience, too. But after three weeks, Mom was still considered comatose. That's when I decided to speak to her candidly about her situation. One night, I pulled a chair close to her bed, and held her hand.

"I said, 'Mom, you have a tough choice to make now. You can leave us if you want to . . . if you're ready. And if you choose to go, Bruce and I and everyone else will understand, and respect your decision. Or, you can decide to stick around in this life, even though it's going to take a lot of work to get yourself back to normal. It'll be a hard recovery, but we'll work it out. It'll be okay. We all love you very much, and will always love you no matter which you choose.' Later that night she made her decision; she came out of the coma."

"Whoa. You just gave me such chills," I said, rubbing my arms. "She definitely heard you."

"Yes she did," Paul said. "And because she showed the will to live, I continued to give her Bio-Touch sessions every day. She grew steadily stronger. But the doctors warned me not to get my hopes up. They were certain she'd never be able to walk or talk again, or ever regain her former mental capabilities. I was tired of their pessimism, though, so I ignored them."

"Why were they so afraid to offer you hope?" I asked.

"Maybe they preferred to deliver bad news, and then look like heroes if things exceeded their expectations. I don't know, but whenever I walked past the waiting room, I saw a never-ending stream of people sitting in fear and despair, hoping for some news about a loved one. It made me realize how lucky I was. I had something I could do for my mother that helped her, but also gave me a sense of power in that difficult situation. I had a measure of control—an unusual thing for a layperson in a medical setting. And that just reinforced my desire to share Bio-Touch with all families, someday.

"Soon Mom was moved out of intensive care and into the cardiac rehabilitation unit of the hospital. That's when the next bomb dropped," Paul said as he threw up his hands. "Her insurance company called to inform us that they were sorry, but Vivian had 'maxed out' her benefits. They said that they were not going to pay more because she was not going to get better. I knew I had another fight on my hands. Not only was I continually pushing to keep the hospital staff interested in my mother's improvement, but now I had to prevent the insurance company from giving up on her, too.

"I began calling her insurance carrier every day, sometimes several times a day, trying to convince them that Mom was really getting better. Eventually the company got tired of hearing from me and promised to keep paying, but only for a while.

"Meanwhile, I worked to convince the doctors to prescribe physical therapy for Mom. But when a physical therapist and an occupational therapist finally arrived to assess her condition, they said her prognosis looked grim. That sounded like a death sentence for my mother—especially the way they said it right in front of her," Paul said with annoyance. "So, I led them out into the hallway, and told them that the last thing we needed was their negative attitudes. I explained how hard I tried to keep the doctors engaged every step of the way. They listened and apologized."

"But did they work with her?"

"Yes, and there were a lot of things Mom had to relearn, especially how to sit up and stand. One of the ways the therapists accomplished that involved strapping her between two boards to build up her strength. They kept her busy for hours each day, while I continued her Bio-Touch sessions. And to the therapists' amazement, Mom worked so hard and progressed so quickly, it didn't take long before she was transferred to a rehabilitation facility.

"It was at that facility that she learned how to walk again. At first, she managed to take two steps. Then, she could take ten. And soon, she was walking twenty steps. She became the 'miracle case' to all those doctors and therapists who insisted she had no chance of recovering any of her former abilities."

"How wonderful. I love hearing those kinds of 'beating-the-odds' stories."

"Yeah, she sure did that. By October, only six weeks after her surgeries, she was sent home. Physical and occupational therapists came to her house to complete her rehabilitation. Cheryl flew to Denver, moving in with Mom, temporarily, to continue Bio-Touch sessions. By the way, it was the first time they ever met. Meanwhile, I flew back to Hawaii to work with Joyzelle at the new Bio-Touch Center."

"What an unusual way to meet your mother-in-law for the first time. Moving in to be her caretaker. Boy, that could have been a volatile situation for some families," I said.

"That's for sure. Luckily, they got along very well. Mom's progress was incredible as she quickly relearned to speak and feed herself. But in November I returned to Denver to help facilitate the sale of her home and business. Even though she was doing well, she certainly wasn't able to work or even to live alone anymore.

"By December, Mom was on a plane with me and Cheryl, flying to her new home in Hawaii. We rented a four-bedroom house in Kailua, located a block from the beach. Joyzelle moved in with us, too. We continued giving Mom Bio-Touch sessions at home and at the center, as well.

"Slowly, she began to understand all that happened to her. She was saddened by her severe limitations. But she was shocked when she realized she lost weeks of her life in a coma, and then awoke unable to move, walk, speak, or feed herself. She was mortified that she was wearing diapers, too. Now that the fog had lifted from her brain, she understood how radically her life changed in an instant."

"That must have been so horrible for her," I said. "Especially since she was fairly young and still active."

"It was terrible. She had such a zest for life; her energy levels were always off the charts. As a young woman she danced professionally with the Ziegfeld Follies in stage shows and movies. She entertained the troops on missions with the United Service Organization (USO) during World War II," Paul said, his voice thick with admiration. "Even as she grew older, she was always on the go, enjoying life, and relishing her independence. But now, Mom struggled to walk fifty feet by herself.

"One day I asked her how she made that tough choice—while still comatose in the hospital—to continue on in this life. She looked at me intently and said, 'Giving up on life wasn't an option for me. That's not the way I was raised. Taking the easy way out would have been considered a failure. And that kind of failure would have been unacceptable.'"

"Unbelievable," I said, my mouth agape. "Isn't it incredible how things drummed into our heads in childhood can influence us decades later—even while in a coma?"

"It is," Paul answered with a nod, "and apparently that's how deeply we're affected by what our parents say to us and expect from us."

"Hmmm . . . because we're in those societal boxes, and not really free, huh?"

Paul smiled. "That's right. Anyway, a year after her surgeries in September of 1992, I took Mom to a new doctor for an electrocardiogram (EKG) to see how her heart was doing. On a normal day, it would have been just a routine checkup. But that day was anything but normal.

Hurricane Iniki was bearing down on the Islands. It kept moving closer to Honolulu all day, and the tourists were in a tizzy. Locals were bracing for disaster by taping and boarding up windows in homes, hotels, and shops. Food and water were flying off the store shelves as people stocked up.

"With all that tension in the air, I expected Mom's heart rate to be erratic during the EKG. It would have been understandable, too, if her blood pressure was high. But not only was her blood pressure perfect, the EKG results were also perfect. The doctor announced that Mom had the heart of a twenty year old! I was so amazed, I burst out laughing. The man looked at me like I was nuts, so I told him that her heart had been punctured by a pacemaker a year ago. Then I filled him in on everything she'd been through.

"The doctor's eyes grew wide with disbelief. He said there were no signs of trauma or damage to her heart, whatsoever, and if there were any, they would have shown up on the EKG. But I just thanked him, and smiled as I helped my mother out the door.

"As we drove along, the wind blew like crazy, and the sky turned dark. But I couldn't get that doctor's shocked expression out of my head, or that smile off my face. And as luck would have it, Hurricane Iniki bypassed Honolulu that day. At the last minute, it changed course and hit Kauai instead. Yes, that was a day I'll never forget."

"That is an astonishing Bio-Touch story, Paul. So, what happened to Vivian as time went on?"

"Mom improved in many ways. She was even able to walk short distances by herself. Her biggest breakthrough happened the day she held my hand as we walked a couple of hundred yards down to the beach. Slowly but surely she got through all that sand so she could stand in the ocean waves. That was a great moment for both of us.

"But she had to work hard to keep up her walking skills. Eventually she decided that she was content to spend most of her time in a wheelchair. We all respected her choice. She was grateful enough to be able to speak clearly, comprehend everything, laugh, and enjoy life, again.

"She wasn't really happy living in Hawaii, though, so she was relieved when we moved to Tucson. Mom bought a house to share with Cheryl, Joyzelle, and me. She lived in good health for another nine years. And until the end, her heart and lungs remained in excellent condition, without medication."

"Paul, during those years, did you two ever talk about your relationship? About the past? About your decision to drop out of society? About her pain when you did?"

"Oh, sure," Paul answered, "but not in an emotionally charged way. It wasn't necessary to discuss it like that. Our relationship was perfect in the present. We loved each other. I was taking care of her with the help of my wife and many of our Bio-Touch friends, just as I promised. You see, years before I moved to the land, I told Mom if she ever needed full-time care someday, she could live with me instead of in an old-age facility. And that's exactly what happened. And it happened because I was in the right place, spiritually, to help her when she needed me."

A feeling of relief washed over me. I was surprised at how happy I was hearing that Paul's relationship with his mom was a loving one, after all.

"Ironically," Paul continued, "the reason I was able to take care of my mother for all those years was because of what I learned from my spiritual studies on the land—how to be free of those limiting roles of society. I learned how to honor my mother for the person she was, not the role she played. And I learned I didn't need to obey and please her to have her love me."

"Well, things sure happened for you as they were supposed to. There's no denying that. And I'm starting to see how, despite the fact that people's feelings got hurt, dropping out of society helped you reach your full potential. It really did pave the way for you to reach your destiny."

Paul nodded. "Exactly. Oh, one more thing," he said as he stood up to leave. "While Mom was in the process of dying, I sat with her in complete, peaceful silence. I knew I was being given the opportunity to reflect on the meaning of birth, life, and death. It was the final lesson a mother could give her son—how to die gracefully. I wrote a poem for her, then."

"May I hear it?" I asked. For some reason, I began to tremble.

Paul remained standing as he recited this poem for his dying mother:

"God bless you, Viv,
God bless you, mother,
You are always a part of me, now.
Thank you for loving me,
Thank you for helping me feel safe,
I love you eternally,
Your son."

My throat tightened as warm tears hit my cheeks. My nose turned liquid. I blinked a few times to bring Paul back into focus. "That was beautiful. Thank you for sharing it with me," I blubbered as I walked him to the door. I gave him a quick hug, keeping my face averted so he wouldn't see it turning into moist mush.

After I closed the door behind him, I really let the waterworks flow. I was a sentimental crybaby, anyway, but that poem really got to me. Although concise, it perfectly captured the emotion surrounding the death of his mother, and his gratitude for her protection and love.

I didn't know why Paul and Vivian's past resonated so deeply within me. Oddly enough, I felt a connection with Vivian—a woman I never met—the very first time Paul mentioned her. Suddenly I was ashamed of the way I had criticized the love and loyalty he had for his mother. Who was I to judge him and try to force their relationship into one of those societal boxes? Riding up there on my high horse, I was clueless about the depth of love and devotion Paul and his mother shared. I just wanted them to fit nicely into my own perception of what was appropriate. Oh well, at least now I could see how judgmental I'd been. Thanks, self-awareness. You sure know how to hold up the mirror of truth—especially when it's painful to peer into it.

CHAPTER THIRTEEN

My Own Experience
with Bio-Touch

A tingly feeling skittered around inside my left hand. Where did that come from all of a sudden? I stopped typing on my computer keyboard to rub away the weird pins-and-needles sensation from my palm, thumb, and fingers. The mini massage helped, temporarily. But as the days passed, the odd prickling intensified. At night, my hand fell asleep long before I could.

Then an achy stiffness, subtle at first, crept around the base of my neck. My shoulders felt like they needed re-alignment. I hoped my issues weren't carpal tunnel syndrome—something my mother had suffered with before undergoing surgery years before.

I tried to pretend those annoyances weren't there, so I wouldn't have to deal with them. But soon it became clear that ignoring them wasn't working. I tried typing less, but that wasn't a productive solution for someone writing a book.

Howard bought a gel-filled wrist support, placing it in front of the keyboard to redistribute my pressure points as I typed. I swallowed nutritional supplements that were supposed to reduce tissue swelling associated with my possible carpal tunnel syndrome. I figured the pills couldn't hurt, and might be an easy fix for my problem. Finally, I did hand and wrist exercises I found online. Obviously, patience was required for any of those remedies to work. Too bad I had none of that; I wanted to feel normal immediately.

One day while giving a Bio-Touch session, I lifted my arms so I could reach my recipient's ears. Suddenly it felt like my hand hit a high voltage wire. A crazy stinging snaked from my fingers to my wrist. I noticed my gripping ability was weaker, too. Uh-oh. I definitely had a problem. As I struggled to finish the session, I wondered if the solution was, indeed, right under my nose.

Paul often nagged me because I didn't receive regular Bio-Touch sessions. In fact, in the three-plus years I volunteered at the center, I had never scheduled an appointment for myself. Paul would say, "Debra, most practitioners come in for weekly sessions. You're the only practitioner who never comes for sessions at all. Why is that?"

"Because I feel fine. Nothing hurts me," was my typical reply.

"Everyone should have Bio-Touch sessions to continue feeling fine," he'd continue. "It's like a maintenance program. You know that by now, don't you?"

"Sure," I'd say. "You're right. I'll make an appointment soon." But I never got around to making that appointment. I knew if I ever really needed a session, any practitioner would be happy to squeeze me in between their scheduled recipients. Well, now I really needed a session.

After my last recipient of the day had gone, I took a deep breath and walked over to where Paul was sitting at the desk. "My hand is tingling badly," I admitted in a low voice. I held my breath as I rubbed my fingers.

He looked at me with raised eyebrows. "Well, Debra," he said with a smile, "it had to happen."

"What do you mean? What had to happen?"

"You had to suffer from something, eventually, so you'd need a Bio-Touch session."

I looked at him as if he was nuts. "Why?"

"Because you're writing a book about Bio-Touch, of course. How can you write from an insightful point of view without having experienced a Bio-Touch session for yourself?"

My jaw dropped, as I was hit full force by the realization. Damn, he was right! It was essential for me to have firsthand knowledge of my subject, so to speak. Why hadn't I thought of that before?

"Come on." He motioned with his hand. "I'll give you a quick session right now."

I hesitated. "I can't remove my shirt for you to work on me."

"Don't worry. I remember your promise to Howard. I can work around your shirt."

I stepped into a session room while Paul went to wash his hands. It felt strange climbing onto the massage table instead of standing next to it. My eyes swept the room focusing on things through a recipient's point of view. The teal wall color surrounded me with a sense of peace, while the soft glow of the corner salt lamp added a warm coziness to the room.

Paul returned, leaving the door wide open for our impromptu session. He moved his hands efficiently around the restraints of my shirt, paying close attention to the back of my neck, even though I hadn't mentioned that it hurt. I realized how stiffly I was holding my head, once his fingers zeroed in. As he swept downward from the base of my skull, the sudden easing of my muscles flooded me with relief. I was embarrassed to hear myself cooing like a contented pigeon.

After working on my neck, he addressed my head. As he touched specific areas, I could feel a light buzzing around my forehead. When Paul worked on my arm and hand, warm blood engorged my icy palm and fingers. It was a strange, but pleasant sensation. Soon a loose heaviness engulfed the entire area from my shoulder to my fingertips.

Nobu, who regularly volunteered on Fridays with us, walked by the session room door. She looked in, stopping in her tracks to stare wide-eyed at us. "Debra's having a Bio-Touch session?" She brought the back of her hand up to her forehead. "I think I'm going to faint," she teased.

"Yes, the day has finally arrived," I said with a sigh.

"About time." She rolled her eyes as she walked on.

Paul continued the session. The tension evaporated from my body; I felt safe. It was as if I was home on a rainy day, curled under a blanket in my favorite chair. He finished, leaving me alone to savor the quiet calm coursing through me. I was tempted to stretch out on the table, cover myself with a sheet, and take a nap. Instead, I walked out to the desk to thank Paul. I felt lighter. I was even smiling as I had seen so many other recipients do after their sessions. I drove home with high hopes.

Throughout the following week, I was happy to notice the tingling in my hand was less severe. Unfortunately, though, the soreness in my neck grew worse. I tried to keep my normal schedule of housework and errands, while avoiding turning my face up or down, or to either side. Instead, I moved my eyeballs, shifting them in their sockets like a ventriloquist's dummy. I moved robot-like, twisting my upper torso and shoulders along with my neck.

My usually peaceful bedtime morphed into a frustrating challenge evaluating an array of pillows to find one that caused the least amount of neck tension. Howard quietly endured that routine, as well as my loud "ows" during the night whenever I turned. Lifting my heavy head off the pillow became an even bigger trial. Anticipating the pain, I had to spend a few minutes psyching myself up first. I just wanted to be hoisted by one of those sturdy crane hooks found on construction sites.

When Friday rolled around again, I arrived at the center early for my shift so Paul could give me a session before my first recipient showed up. Again, he worked on my throbbing neck for quite a while before moving to my hand and arm. Right away everything felt looser and lighter. I was thrilled to be able to work on my recipients with less discomfort that entire afternoon. I enjoyed going out to dinner and the symphony with Howard and our friends that evening. And I slept well that night.

In the morning, after I delayed the moment as long as possible, I lifted my head off the pillow and felt . . . nothing. Hooray! But I wanted to test it out just to be sure, so I lowered my head onto the pillow, waited a few seconds, and lifted it again. There was no pain.

My first thought was how relieved I was to have my normal, pain-free existence back. Then I was amazed that Bio-Touch really worked. But why was I so surprised? For years, I saw the way recipients were helped and heard many uplifting Bio-Touch stories. So how could I still be uncertain about the healing technique I regularly shared with others? Why did I still harbor some absence of faith? As I berated myself, I remembered how Paul had admitted to having his own doubts about Bio-Touch through the years. It had proven itself to him in the end, though. Now it had proven itself to me.

My neck still felt a bit tight on the left side, and my hand still tingled occasionally. But they were much better than they had been, so I could forget about them for hours at a time. Paul worked on me five straight weeks—one session per week—and at the end of that time, my neck was completely loose and pain-free, my hand was tingle-free, and I had regained normal range of motion.

I know there are other effective touch-healing methods out there. Recently I read about one in which the practitioners have to breathe certain ways, and create energy fields with their minds before and during sessions. I'm sure those techniques help people, but they sound like a lot of effort for the practitioner. Bio-Touch is simple. I just touch. While working on a recipient, I can inhale or exhale, as I need to. I can think about what I'm making for dinner, how frustrated I am with the price of gasoline, or absolutely nothing at all. It doesn't matter. My touch, alone, is effective. And so is everybody else's.

Bio-Touch gave me a tool to help people feel better, which was what I was compelled to find after Jill's illness. It also helped me heal physically, alleviating my neck and hand issues, as well as emotionally. The sharp pain of mourning I carried around in my heart for years had dulled to a reasonable ache. Bio-Touch was the healing salve, letting me feel cared for while receiving a session, and helping me to connect with others while giving a session. Paul explained it best when he said, "Bio-Touch is love, and love is Bio-Touch."

So, I'll continue to volunteer at the Bio-Touch Center, giving sessions to my recipients and rejoicing with them when their pains and discomforts fade away. I'll keep offering sessions to family and friends in need, too, and even to strangers if the situation arises.

While writing this book, I realized that Paul is not just my fellow Bio-Touch practitioner, friend, and spiritual sibling. He's also my mentor. Just as Janet taught me about the unseen world of spirit and soul years ago, Paul has been my teacher over the past four years, helping me learn more about myself than I ever wanted to know.

I have no idea where the path I'm on will lead me. I hope it's a place where I'll gain an even greater understanding of my strengths, weaknesses, thoughts, and emotions, and how they affect me and the people around me. And that's what embodies the most important aspect of Bio-Touch. Self-awareness. Finally, I get it!

Words from Paul Bucky

This book is a dance. Its steps and movements come together the same way that Debra shares her life's path and her experiences with Bio-Touch. I am enthralled to realize how the history of Bio-Touch, Debra's life, and my own personal journey mesh together in such perfect harmony. Each meeting we had to discuss my past gave me a new awareness of myself, as I also learned of Debra's past. I have come to realize how each of our personal journeys is so intertwined with others. There is merely the finest thread of individualization.

Through the process of watching Debra create this book, I have also learned how we truly are all one, and my awe at the magical expression of the oneness we experience when practicing Bio-Touch has been reignited.

Thank you, Debra, for opening your heart to us. Thank you for letting yourself be loved, and thank you for loving us.

Afterword

Carole A. McKenzie, PhD, CNM, RN

Associate Professor of Nursing, Texas A&M University Commerce

The book you have just read discusses the first person experience of someone who embraced the complementary energy therapy, Bio-Touch. It also includes anecdotal and research information from practitioners who have utilized Bio-Touch and have seen the difference it can make in anybody's life. It also recounts how Bio-Touch came into being and the impact it has had on not only individuals, but health care education programs and communities.

As a health care professional, I constantly look for ways to improve health care for my clients and to teach my students to provide care that is holistic and has few side effects. I discovered Bio-Touch through a colleague, and it clearly met those requirements.

I was instantly intrigued and felt a total connection to it. I began with taking the Bio-Touch class and then began having my students take the class. Eventually, I had my students take the beginning and advanced classes, and then had students in research class conduct pre- and post-intervention research using Bio-Touch. The results were astounding. We had large convenience samples showing improvement in all areas, including reduction of pain, stress, and restlessness, and improvement of feelings of well-being and relaxation. Finally, we did measurements of pre- and post-blood pressures, pulse, and respiration. Improvement was noted in all areas on a sample size of 202.

While it was clear subjectively that Bio-Touch made a difference, the various studies conducted indicated objective, marked improvement in all areas. Since there are no side effects and no special equipment required, most components can be performed anywhere, and

Bio-Touch is so easy to learn that children can be taught, so there is no down side.

Because Bio-Touch has an impact on decreasing stress and improving health outcomes, one can make the case that for clients who are receiving Bio-Touch, their productivity is enhanced—making it a cost-saving measure. There is also limited research indicating that immunity is improved. That connection is difficult to prove, given the cost of applicable research, but it certainly makes reasonable scientific sense. Again, if managing stress is one of the preventative strategies to manage illness, the cost and wellness benefits of Bio-Touch are important.

The amazing thing about Bio-Touch is that it is easily incorporated into any training program, and even lay persons can be taught the methods at health fairs and any public venue. When I was the director of a nursing program, we required all students to take the beginning and advanced courses and to utilize it with clients, teach it at health fairs, and conduct research on it. It is incredibly important to me that students incorporate holistic, complementary strategies into their client care. Bio-Touch is an important and easy way to accomplish this.

As a nurse, a nurse midwife, a clinical specialist, and a faculty member, I live the belief that any approach that strengthens clients and their ability to gain the most optimal health outcomes is worthwhile. The bonus, in the case of Bio-Touch, is that no harm can be done.

Additionally, Bio-Touch has brought together colleagues who are really more like family united by a common belief and openness to using any strategy that works, regardless of its origins. Those colleagues promote and sustain an organization supporting Bio-Touch that is nonprofit in nature and dedicated to helping others.

It continues to surprise most people that such a simple approach can make such a difference. Students, faculty, and clients provided additional anecdotal examples of how effective Bio-Touch was and how well it was received by those who utilized it. The other thing that was critical to me is the belief that touching has to be an integral part of providing client care. Over the years, the concept of touching has had a negative connotation to some professionals and their clients. I saw Bio-Touch as a simple and effective way to "reclaim" touch for health care providers. I encourage anyone who is looking for ways to provide better care to clients to investigate, learn, and utilize Bio-Touch. You'll be convinced of its merits.

Because the education necessary to deliver the techniques of Bio-Touch requires a minimum of time, it can easily be incorporated as part of the holistic thread of any health care curriculum or as part of staff development. Promoting the best possible health outcomes is a key responsibility of health care providers. I believe that Bio-Touch is one of the most efficacious ways to accomplish this.

Acknowledgments

I wish to thank Howard, my husband, my rock and the love of my life, for his patience, immense encouragement, and unwavering support. I'm so lucky to have him by my side on all the journeys of my life.

A special thank you goes to our daughter, Jill, whose pain compelled me to find Bio-Touch in the first place. She's always believed in my writing ability, and encouraged me every step of the way.

I'm so grateful to David, our son, for his special kind of encouragement, and for using his unique ability to deliver comic relief whenever I needed a laugh.

Thank you to my mother, Gertrude NuDell Gordon, who is, and has always been, the number one fan of my writing. She has nurtured my love of words from the day she climbed into bed with me to read *Cinderella*. It's my earliest and fondest memory.

Thank you to my sister, Mel Fink, who has always encouraged me to spread my wings and try something new . . . like writing a book.

Thank you to Pesi Dinnerstein, whose friendship, encouragement, advice, and support has meant so much to me. A published author herself, she helped me see myself that way.

I'm grateful to Sheri and Dave Wechsler for their loving friendship and rock-solid support. Their faith in me is a precious gift.

I wish to thank Cheryl Bucky for the hours she spent talking into my tape recorder. She graciously allowed me to peer through the window of her fascinating past, providing crucial details about her years with Paul and Bio-Touch.

I wish to thank everyone associated with the Bio-Touch organization for their support and encouragement. The following people are the biggest of my Bio-Touch family cheerleaders: Lila and Irv Berman, Missy Jewell, Michael Plumb, Edwin Monier, Cheryl Hackett, Bev Wood, Chardonai, and Soledad and John Cooper. Sadly, John Cooper passed away, but I'll always treasure how happy and excited he was that I was writing this book.

Thank you to Robie Jean Chandler. She was the first person at the Bio-Touch Center to gently and lovingly pierce the protective shield I'd surrounded myself with, sensing how much I needed her to.

Thank you to Carol Galuskin and Lisa Shiva for being such amazing listeners. I could always count on their unwavering support and enthusiasm for the book.

I wish to thank Ethel Lee Miller, Nan Andres, Bill Black, and the other members of the Sunset Writers Group of Tucson, Arizona, for their expert feedback, suggestions, and encouragement over the years as they read sections of the manuscript.

With all my heart, I'd like to thank my literary agent, Bill Gladstone. He took a chance on a new writer, recognizing Bio-Touch's potential to relieve the pain, stress, and misery of so many people around the world.

A huge thank you goes to Dr. Gary Schwartz for writing the foreword to this book. He has believed in the power of Bio-Touch for years, having researched its merits for himself. His encouragement, after reading my raw manuscript, meant the world to me.

Another huge thank you goes to Dr. Carole McKenzie, for writing the afterword to this book. She has been an ardent supporter of Bio-Touch for many years, introducing it into the curriculum at Northwestern Oklahoma State University's school of nursing and leading her students in research projects proving its effectiveness.

I am deeply grateful to Kenzi Sugihara, Nancy Sugihara, my awesome editor; and Kenichi Sugihara. Their experience, talent, and insight have made my first book publishing experience more pleasurable than I could have imagined.

And finally, how do I find the words to thank my dear friend and soul sibling, Paul Bucky? With the patience of a saint, he allowed me to interview him in depth, sitting for hours reliving and relaying the incredible story of his past. Often he had to explain his actions and thought processes repeatedly until they made sense to me. Always my spiritual mentor, he used examples of his life to illustrate the points he deemed important for me to understand. For all his contributions to this book, as well as to my spiritual growth, I will be forever grateful.

About the Author

Photo by Jennifer Vimmerstedt

DEBRA SCHILDHOUSE was born and raised in Cincinnati, Ohio. She attended the University of Cincinnati, where she met her husband, Howard. Relishing a traditional marriage, she enjoyed being a stay-at-home mom to their two children. For many years she spent her spare time volunteering for numerous organizations as well as her children's schools.

After watching a movie about touch-healing in 1980, Debra became fascinated with the subject, and began "healing" friends and family, drawing upon the energy in her fingers. When that method failed to ease the pain and other symptoms her daughter suffered during a bout of viral meningitis, Debra searched for a technique she could count on. Her search ended when she discovered Bio-Touch.

Debra is a certified practitioner of Bio-Touch™, and has been a volunteer staff member at the Bio-Touch Center in Tucson, Arizona for over five years. She is also a member of the Board of Directors of the International Foundation of Bio-Magnetics (IFBM), which is the educational arm of the Bio-Touch organization. She writes articles, newsletters, and website content for IFBM.

In addition to writing, Debra enjoys reading, baking, listening to classical music, and spending time with her family.

More About Bio-Touch

It is Your Birthright to Be Healthy, Happy, and Loved!

What is Bio-Touch?

Bio-Touch consists of lightly touching (butterfly-like) specific points on the body. The combination of correct points and light touch enhances the body's natural healing ability.

Taught Through an Education and Charitable Foundation

Bio-Touch is taught through the International Foundation of Bio-Magnetics (IFBM), a federally approved 501(c)3 education and charitable foundation. Certified practitioners provide Bio-Touch sessions at the Bio-Touch Center in Tucson, Arizona, on a donation basis to anyone in need of relief from pain, stress, or symptoms of disease. All certified practitioners on staff at the center are volunteers.

IFBM'S **Mission** is to teach Bio-Touch, an application of the universal principle "Love thy Neighbor," as a means to alleviate pain and stress, and support good health through all stages of life.

IFBM'S **Vision** is to encourage all people to take responsibility for their own health care, empower them to assist others, and create a community of people worldwide dedicated to service, self-awareness, and recognizing the equality of all humanity—thus forming a chain which shall go on indefinitely.

Anyone Can Learn Bio-Touch

꙰ It is **easy to learn**—in fact, so easy that *even children can learn and practice it effectively!*

꙰ Research shows that Bio-Touch significantly *reduces stress levels.*

꙰ There are *no philosophies or beliefs to adopt, no masters or gurus to train under, and no levels of achievement to attain.*

꙰ It is the *perfect complement to any healthcare program,* bodywork therapy, or standard medical protocol.

You Can Learn Bio-Touch Now

Download the **FREE preview of the Bio-Touch training manual** at
www.justtouch.com/free-preview-copy-of-ebook.

OR

Join Bio-Touch for *$18 for a one-year membership* and receive
a FREE *copy of the full download version of the training manual*
at www.justtouch.com/member.

More Resources on the Bio-Touch Website

There is a wealth of information about Bio-Touch on its website at
www.justtouch.com.

꙰ The *Health Conditions* page addresses the application of Bio-Touch as a healing touch technique for over 50 specific health conditions.

꙰ The *Research* page has research, PowerPoint presentations, and papers.

꙰ The *Class Registration* page lists classes and workshops available online and at the Bio-Touch Center in Tucson, Arizona.

꙰ The *Media* page includes a number of first-person videos discussing Bio-Touch.

And you can purchase *Awakening Athena: Resilience, Restoration and Rejuvenation for Women*, written by Kenna Stephenson, M.D., which includes a chapter about Bio-Touch. Dr. Stephenson was the principal investigator on a Bio-Touch research project at the University of Texas Health Center in Tyler, Texas. In 2003 Dr. Stephenson gave a presentation on Bio-Touch at the national conference of the American Association of Integrative Medicine. According to Dr. Stephenson, "Bio-Touch provides a valuable modality for pain and stress reduction. Many patients in my practice have benefitted from Bio-Touch for stress related disorders. . . . Our research confirms that Bio-Touch has an immediate and sustained favorable effect on bodily pain and physical functioning in addition to an overall improvement in Quality of Life Scores in patients."

IFBM
5634 E Pima St
Tucson AZ 85749
520.323.7951 or 800.473.3812
www.justtouch.com

Printed in Great Britain
by Amazon

40772893R00126